Lone Star Dinosaurs

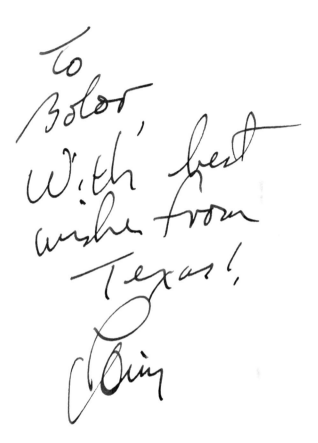

To Bolor,
With best
wishes from
Texas!,

NUMBER TWENTY-TWO:
*Louise Lindsey Merrick
Natural Environment Series*

Lone Star
DINOSAURS

by Louis Jacobs

Original artwork by Karen Carr

Texas A&M University Press • College Station

Design adapted from Ralph C. Gauer, Jr.

The paper used in this book meets the minimum requirements
of the American National Standard for Permanence
of Paper for Printed Library Materials, Z39.48-1984.
Binding materials have been chosen for durability.

∞

Library of Congress Cataloging-in-Publication Data

Jacobs, Louis L.
    Lone Star dinosaurs / by Louis Jacobs ; original artwork by
Karen Carr. —1st ed.
        p.   cm. — (Louise Lindsey Merrick natural environment
series ; no. 22)
    Includes bibliographical references and index.
    ISBN 0-89096-662-1 (alk. paper)
    1. Dinosaurs—Texas.   I. Title.   II. Series.
QE862.D5J285   1995   95-4034
567.9'1'09764—dc20   CIP

To Wann Langston, Jr., professor emeritus
of the University of Texas at Austin,
who exemplifies professional paleontologists;

to Kathy Poff, teacher at Parkhill Junior High School,
Richardson Independent School District,
who exemplifies teachers;

and to my children, Matthew and Melissa,
who exemplify school kids,
some of whom will become scientists,
all of whom like dinosaurs.

What a glorious continuity of the mind.

Contents

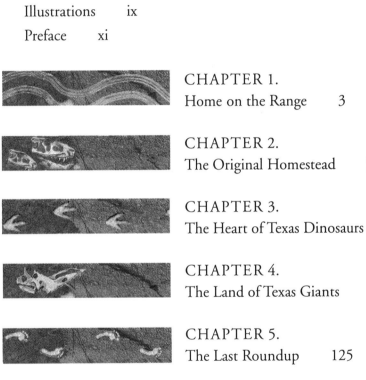

Illustrations

Preface

These are exciting times in paleontology. So many new discoveries are being made; so many new ways of looking at fossils are being devised. The fossils of the Lone Star State have much to contribute to the fervor. That is why it is so exciting for me to have the opportunity to write this book, although I know—and even hope—that time and future discoveries will markedly change our perception of dinosaurs as I have written about them. Time and future discoveries will not, however, change the almost universal appeal of dinosaurs, especially when those dinosaurs tell a story that hits so close to home.

There are other reasons why I am excited about this book. I am a descendant of one of Austin's Old Three Hundred pioneer settlers. Another of my ancestors was a volunteer who fought with Fannin's Georgia Battalion in the Texas Revolution and was captured at the Battle of Goliad. Later he was a veteran of the Somervell and Mier expeditions to Mexico, was captured again, and held prisoner until he escaped from the Castle of San Carlos de Perote. One of his sons was a deputy marshal of the Paris (Texas) court. He was shot and killed on a train crossing the Red River. So, you see, I have a stake in Texas history, and I especially like the idea of visiting its remote and ancient roots. I am excited to have the chance to write (in chapter 2) about studies done earlier this century at Smithers Lake in Fort Bend County. My great-great-grandfather's house is now a part of the Fort Bend County Museum. Writing this book has been a personal, as well as a professional, experience for me. And it has been fun.

The story begins with the history of vertebrate fossil collecting in Texas and with the people who did the digging. Chapter 1 also details where dinosaurs are found in Texas, how we know how old they are, and why they are important. The next three chapters present the story of Texas dinosaurs region by region, from oldest to youngest, and the threads that bind them together. The closing chapter looks into the thorny problem of extinction and examines dinosaurs as living animals.

One of the reasons paleontology is fun is because of the people with whom you get to work. Fieldwork builds strong bonds. The students and professionals of the Shuler Museum of Paleontology at SMU rank at the top. Thanks go to

Eric Ahlstrand, Brian Andres, Anthony Aramoonie, Robert Beauford, Lee Bumpas, Amy Busby, Roland Castenada II, Will Downs (homebased at Northern Arizona University), Alana Everitt, Contessa Fincher, Dina Franco, Elizabeth Gomani, Jonathan Helwig, Brad Hood, Adrienne King, Jennifer Kohl, Andrew Konnerth, Mike Lee, Yuong-Nam Lee, Steve Mahoney, Carlos Maldonado, David and Kecia Maldonado, Dana March, Amal Mohamed, Mike Moreno, Kent Newman (who teaches at Wilson Middle School, Plano Independent School District), Arnold Palmer, Dee Dee Pargman, Paul Pinter, Ginny Rence, Kirk Rothemund, Tracy Sole, Todd Ventura, Patricia Whalen, Jack Whittles, Dale and Alisa Winkler, Xu Xiaofeng, and Vicki Yarborough. Phillip A. Murry of Tarleton State University and a progression of his students—Michelle Bandt, Alan Barck, James R. Branch (now a graduate student at Baylor), Tracy Edwards, Henry Huggins, Jim Leatherwood, Rachel Moravek, Cindy Ridgway, Sharon Turner, Patrick Trudell (who later came to SMU), and Richard Wolfe—have long been collaborators in the investigation of Texas dinosaurs. Jeffrey G. Pittman of East Texas State University shared his knowledge of dinosaur footprints. He and his students—Scott Brown, Valerie Cheshier, Ronnie Freeman, Jeff Haynes, Kevin Hill, Lee O'Neal, Robert Pitt, Randy Stephens, Jennifer Turley, and Austin Williams—are fine colleagues in the field.

Wann Langston, Jr., Ernest Lundelius, and Melissa Winans facilitated use of the vertebrate paleontology collections of the Texas Memorial Museum at the J. J. Pickle Research Station of the University of Texas. Sankar Chatterjee showed me the exciting fossils from the Post Quarry and other specimens housed at the Museum of Texas Tech University. Billy Paul Baker and the staff at Dinosaur Valley State Park have been extremely helpful. The U.S. Army Corps of Engineers has facilitated work at Proctor Lake and Lake Grapevine.

It is a pleasure to work with museums that take the results of university research and present them to the public in exciting ways. Don Otto and his staff at the Fort Worth Museum of Science and History have taken a leading role in expediting paleontology in North Texas with exemplary results. They are a great bunch of people, but I wish to single out Jim Diffily specifically, because he is an able field companion with boundless enthusiasm for natural history and a good heart. I also thank Henry Schulson, director of the Dallas Museum of Natural History, for his part in our joint paleontological efforts.

I thank all the dinosaur enthusiasts who have helped by making their discoveries available and in sharing their knowledge of local areas. Among these are Johnny Byers, Gary Byrd, Cameron Campbell, Mark Cohen, Ed and Nancy Emborsky, Roger Farish, Lloyd Hill, Sam and Becky Liberato, Bill Lowe, John and Johnny Maurice, John Moody, Arlene Pike, Mike and Sandy Polcyn, Rob

Reid, Ken Smith, Gary Spaulding, Chris and Stormy Wadleigh, Thad Williams and his family, and Richard and Shawn Zack. Most of these enthusiasts are members of the Dallas Paleontological Society. Brad McCormick of the Paleontological Research Institute provided useful specimens. Landowners with whom I have enjoyed working include James and Dorothy Doss, James Graves, Philip Hobson, William W. Jones, and their families. My contacts with public school officials and with teachers, especially Sherrie Prague of the Irving Independent School District and James McConnell of the Richardson Independent School District, have helped me gauge this work. I also want to thank Jake Goree, my son's friend who likes baseball and dinosaurs, for his interest and his questions. All these people deserve credit because they all are dedicated to paleontology and to learning and have helped me develop this story of Texas dinosaurs.

In the course of writing I have spoken with Glen Evans, Joseph T. Gregory, Wann Langston, Jr., Grayson Meade, Donald E. Savage, and John A. Wilson, all of whom have first-hand knowledge of important events in Texas paleontology. David Meltzer provided additional historical information. Christopher R. Cunningham brought me up to date on paleontological developments at the Houston Museum of Natural Science. Christopher Scotese answered my queries about ancient geography. Hilde Schwartz was extremely generous in allowing me access to her excellent work on the Ghost Ranch Quarry. I was afforded the opportunity of examining Ghost Ranch while teaching at SMU's Fort Burgwin Research Center near Taos, New Mexico. Bonnie Jacobs, a paleobotanist (and my wife), advised me on fossil plants.

The entire manuscript was read by Bonnie, by Dale Winkler (my colleague in the office next door), and by Jason Head of the University of Michigan. Various chapters were read by Sankar Chatterjee, Glen Evans, Thor A. Hansen, Wann Langston, Jr., Thomas M. Lehman, and Phillip A. Murry. Their comments were universally helpful and constructive.

The original artwork was rendered with ebullient realism by Karen Carr. Working with her has been a pleasure. Some of the illustrations are from paintings that she did for the Fort Worth Museum of Science and History when they hosted the Dinosaur Society exhibit *The Dinosaurs of Jurassic Park*. Photographs are reproduced courtesy of DeGolyer Library, Southern Methodist University, Dallas, the American Museum of Natural History, and the Panhandle-Plains Museum, Canyon.

Obtaining funds for paleontological projects, as for everything else, is always a struggle. My part of the research on which this book is based has been supported by the National Science Foundation, the National Geographic Society, the Dinosaur Society, the Petroleum Research Fund of the American

Chemical Society, the Institute for the Study of Earth and Man, the Carl B. and Florence E. King Foundation, Southern Methodist University, and the Saurus Institute. Computer Support Corporation, developers of the excellent *Arts and Letters* family of software, has been extraordinarily helpful. Half Price Books, Records and Magazines, through the good offices of Steve Leach, has facilitated this work. I would particularly like to acknowledge the longtime support and friendship of James E. Brooks, president of the Institute for the Study of Earth and Man. I would also like to specifically thank Frederick Schoeller and Louis H. Taylor, both directors of the Saurus Institute. To give back from whence it came, part of the proceeds from this book will go to the Saurus Institute to support dinosaur research.

Finally, I would like to acknowledge my family, for all the reasons that anyone with a family knows.

Yes, these really are exciting times in paleontology. But I have always thought that. When I was a graduate student, all aglow with enthusiasm for whatever project I was working on, I chirped those sentiments to George Gaylord Simpson, one of the truly great paleontologists of this century. He looked at me emotionlessly and said, "All times are exciting in paleontology." He was right, but so was I, and now I know what he meant. These times and all times are exciting for me and other adults, just as they are for today's students, and just as other days will be for tomorrow's. It goes on and on. They may be extinct, but in our minds, dinosaurs—like the great notions they are—keep coming back.

Lone Star Dinosaurs

CHAPTER 1

Home on the Range

MUD COMES IN AN AMAZING variety of textures. On that one day eons ago—one day not lost to the past—the mud was deep but firm. It was a clean mud. It was not too soupy. It was perfect.

A herd of twenty-ton *Pleurocoelus* (PLOOR-uh-SEEL-us), big quadrupedal plant-eating dinosaurs, sauntered across the wet mud flats. Their feet sank eighteen inches into the substrate. The mud sucked at their fleshy soles to hold them tight, but the size of the brontosaurs was accompanied by a fitting strength. Their legs barely felt the tug of earth.

The salt water where the dinosaurs walked was just a few inches deep. On one side the beasts could see the calm blue of the warm lagoonal sea stretching without limit to the horizon. On the other they saw the tall, spidery-leafed conifers, erect on the flat landscape. Dark green cycads and ferns grew in the understory. Flowers were small and grew in bashful patches. With all the trees to hinder their way up from the shore, it is no surprise that the dinosaurs chose to walk on the broad tidal flat, their thunderous feet plodding gently down on the cool, cushioning sediment. The flats provided a comfortable highway, an easy walk with a clear view. The water felt good as it dripped from their rotund bellies and splashed their columnar legs.

That fleeting moment on that particular day—the one that time did not forget—occurred 111 million years ago, deep in the heart of Texas. An instant in the life of dinosaurs was frozen in stone. Footprints left by those magnificent creatures are found all over Central Texas, but the best place to see them is at Dinosaur Valley State Park in Somervell County near the town of Glen Rose, a relaxing sixty-mile drive southwest of Fort Worth through

Pleurocoelus along the shore of the ancient sea that inundated what is now Texas when dinosaurs ruled the Earth. Illustration by Karen Carr, courtesy Fort Worth Museum of Science and History.

grassy prairies and wooded valleys. Glen Rose and the park lie along the Paluxy River, a swiftly flowing tributary of the Brazos. Today, after mountains of time have passed, the rapid waters of the Paluxy apply their energy to removing sediments, now turned to stone, that were deposited in the shallow seas in the days of the dinosaurs. As the river erodes the ancient rock that forms its banks and bed, the footprints made so long ago are illuminated by sunlight once more. Now kids pronk along the walkways where dinosaurs did not fear to tread.

Roland T. Bird—known as R. T. to his friends—built the legacy of dinosaur tracks in Texas. Three-toed dinosaur prints were common along the Paluxy, and they were well known to the moonshiners and fishermen of the region long ago. Charlie Moss found them first, so one story goes, while he was looking for a new site to set up his still. Mabel Adams tells it differently. She was married to Ernest "Bull" Adams, an Oxford-educated Rhodes Scholar and a country lawyer. He was a big man, earning his nickname from his days on the Baylor University football team. Bull put on his shoes and dressed up whenever he was called to Waco to defend a moonshiner. At 103 years of age, Mrs. Adams said in an interview that Bull's brother George found the first tracks. Bull, educated as he was, identified them as dinosaur.

A couple of scientific papers had been written about the Paluxy three-toed tracks before Bird got there. But Bird was more interested in the larger impressions in the river valley, the ones the size of washtubs. They were obviously something. Bird saw them for what they are: tracks of brontosaurs (sauropods more properly), the largest of the land-dwelling animals of their day. This was the first time incontrovertible sauropod tracks had ever been recognized—anywhere. It was a real scientific discovery. Bird made it known to the public.

Bird was at Glen Rose because he was searching for fossils for his boss, Barnum Brown of the American Museum of Natural History in New York. That was his job, and what a great one it must have been. A native of New York, Bird as a young man traveled the American West and Mexico on his Harley-Davidson motorcycle. The fortuitous find of an ancient amphibian while he was setting up camp in Arizona in 1932 catalyzed his relationship with Brown and the American Museum. Brown liked dinosaurs, and he liked their footprints. So in 1938, R. T., as Brown's field collector, ended up in Texas, tracking dinosaurs.

It was the result of an amazing sequence of events. Bird was sent to Gallup, New Mexico, to crate a fossil plant and ship it to New York. While completing his assigned task, he was told that some strange footprints resided in the window of a trading post across town. As snow began to fall, he walked down to see if the story was true. It was. There were footprints, but unfortunately what he saw was not real. They were fakes carved into rock brought to New Mexico from Texas. Frustrated but not discouraged, Bird ferreted on, knowing that there were real prints in the Texas county from which those had been brought. He decided to take the southern route back to New York so he could survey the situation for himself. What else could he do? He was a fossil hunter, so naturally he had to check it out.

The first track he found at Glen Rose was that of a three-toed, medium-sized, meat-eating dinosaur in a block of limestone incorporated into the bandstand at the Somervell County courthouse. It was right there along with hunks of petrified wood, a fossil so common in the region it was sometimes used as building stone. Residents of the area showed him more of the three-toed tracks along the Paluxy. It was while cleaning mud out of these that he noticed a three-foot-long sauropod footprint.

His discovery caused quite a stir with his boss in New York. Arrangements were made to work in cooperation with the Texas Statewide

Tommy Pendley, sitting in a sauropod hind footprint excavated by R. T. Bird. Neg. no. 319835. Photo. R.T. Bird, courtesy Department of Library Services, American Museum of Natural History, New York.

Paleontological Survey being organized by Dr. E. H. Sellards of the University of Texas. The results of the cooperative effort would be shared by the university and the American Museum. It was not until 1940, however, that Bird got back to Texas to work in earnest. He was met in Austin by Glen Evans, one of several young and enthusiastic paleontologists working for Sellards. Evans was familiar with Texas dinosaur tracks from his work as a geologist.

Prints of sauropods and three-toed theropods were dug up by the sweat of a Works Progress Administration (WPA) labor gang working with the State-wide Paleontological Survey. Blocks of limestone with the images of dinosaur feet impressed in them were numbered and hauled to Galveston, where they were loaded onto a steamer and shipped to New York. Shipping them by

Footprints in the bed of the Paluxy River were excavated by Works Progress Administration labor gangs. Cofferdams were built to keep the excavations dry. The trackway being excavated shows three-toed carnivorous dinosaur tracks alongside large sauropod tracks. Neg. No. 128434 Photo. R. T. Bird, courtesy Department of Library Services, American Museum of Natural History, New York.

Occasionally the Paluxy flooded, destroying cofferdams and setting back the work, but Bird and his crew persisted, even in knee-deep water.

steamer worried Bird. Although the United States was not yet at war, German submarines were patrolling the Gulf Stream and could easily torpedo the vessel, a situation that would be undesirable for many more reasons than just simply the loss of the tracks. Fortunately, that did not happen. Safe in New York, the dinosaur trackways were assembled beneath an *Apatosaurus* (uh-PAT-uh-SAWR-us) and an *Allosaurus* (AL-uh-SAWR-us) as if those two had made them. Of course, the Glen Rose footprints were left thirty-five million years after those two dinosaurs had lived, and *Apatosaurus* and *Allosaurus* are not found in Texas anyway. But the footprints made a point in the exhibit: dinosaurs were real animals that moved about and lived and breathed. Through their footprints preserved along that Texas river, they left the evidence of their vitality. Other parts of trackways excavated by Bird went to the University of Texas, Southern Methodist University, Baylor University, the U.S. National Museum, and Brooklyn College.

What about the fakes Bird saw in New Mexico? In Somervell County where the real tracks occur, all the work was hard and hot. To earn some extra cash, local residents turned to moonshining, cutting cedar posts, or digging up dinosaur tracks for sale. Digging up the tracks was hard work and the returns were low. So some back-country entrepreneurs took a shortcut: they carved new prints. Perhaps some of those went to New Mexico along with a few real ones. To a discerning eye, however, forgeries are easily distinguished from the real thing.

Of all the dinosaur prints he found, Bird was particularly interested in a set of parallel trackways: one of a sauropod and the other of a flesh-eating theropod. He must have had a glint in his eye as he wrote in *National Geographic* his vision of the life that produced the Paluxy trackways:

> The huge brontosaur . . . had attracted the attention of a carnivore lurking on near-by land. There [was] the crash of jungle underbrush, the pound of heavy feet . . . a chase was on! . . . The brontosaur, great black flanks and belly streaming water, [weaved its] long neck as it tried to escape an openmouthed lunge of the powerful killer. . . . All would be over if those dagger teeth should grip a point behind the brontosaur's snakelike head.

Maybe that is how it was for a fleeting instant. It is a scenario that we can only imagine. Still, much has been learned about dinosaurs in the past few years, and the visions of these animals have changed because of a better scientific understanding of them. But the excitement over them has not diminished with an increase in knowledge—it has only heated up. And it is not limited to the way dinosaurs were millions of years ago. After reading *Jurassic Park* and seeing the movie, who can think of dinosaurs without DNA, the very symbol of modern science, coming into the picture? Dinosaurs make science exciting. And Texas dinosaurs are beginning to come into their own as never before.

Texas has a wealth of dinosaurs. That is what this book is about. They occur primarily in three areas: Central Texas, where the dinosaurs range from about 115 million to 95 million years old; Big Bend, where dinosaurs lived right up to their demise about 66 million years ago; and the Texas Panhandle around Amarillo, Lubbock, and Big Spring, where dinosaurs over 200 mil-

R. T. Bird could see in his mind a struggle of predator and prey in the days of the dinosaurs. Illustration by Karen Carr.

lion years old are found. Each of these areas tells a different story about dinosaurs, and each has its own story of how dinosaurs were found there.

The discovery of Texas dinosaurs was made by Robert T. Hill. He was not a native Texan, having moved after the Civil War at the age of sixteen, to the Central Texas town of Comanche, in the county of the same name. Hill grew to be crusty and indomitable, a quintessential Texan—if not by birth or in height, at least by inclination. His photographs show piercing eyes and a sometimes dapper flair, traded for grit in the field. He is known as the father of Texas geology because he mapped a large portion of this huge state, studied its fossils, evaluated its artesian springs, and determined the age of many of its rocks. His life in Comanche was spent as a cowboy, a surveyor, and in the printing business. Hill started as a printer's devil—a flunky—for his brother who ran the *Comanche Chief,* eventually working up to more responsible positions. His exercise of responsibility resulted in some friction between the brothers, a foreshadowing of his interpersonal relationships for the rest of his life. While working for the newspaper, he began to frequent Round Mountain and other buttes in the area, collecting fossils and cultivating his love of geology. To pursue this avocation further, he went off to college at Cornell (where he had difficulty graduating). With him went his collection of fossils: mainly the shells of ocean-dwelling animals, but also two "saurian teeth." If those two teeth—found sometime in the late 1870s and now lost—were re-

R. T. Bird in his later years at Dinosaur Valley State Park, where he did the work that made the Paluxy River and Glen Rose famous among paleontologists and dinosaur enthusiasts the world over. He is in front of a model brontosaur. In a strange bit of historical irony, tracks from Glen Rose went to New York and models of T. rex *and* Apatosaurus *were brought to the park in Texas from the 1964 New York World's Fair.*

Jurassic Triassic Cretaceous

Texas has a wealth of dinosaurs. They are found primarily in three big areas: the Panhandle, Central Texas, and Big Bend, wherever continental rocks of the Age of Dinosaurs are found. Areas covered by the sea lacked dinosaurs, but have an abundance of marine fossils. The geologic time scale indicates how old the dinosaurs are in different regions of the state. Illustration by Karen Carr.

ally dinosaur teeth, they very likely are the first dinosaur fossils to be found in Texas.

My reading of Hill is that he was a straight-shooter, committed to hard work and scrupulously honest, and he assumed that others were the same. He was intolerant, if not personally affronted, when they appeared to him not to be as he was (and some of his associates clearly were not). He was disinclined to compromise. Neither of those characteristics did him much good. He had a knack for falling out with people. He worked for the United States Geological Survey, founded the Texas Geological Survey, and was the first professor of geology at the University of Texas. He fell out with them all. He was married three times. He was swindled in two Mexican mining deals and went broke again on gold prospects in Nevada. One of Hill's major contributions to his profession was being the first geologist to report on the

Robert T. Hill, the father of Texas geology and scientific discoverer of dinosaurs in Texas. He had piercing eyes and a dapper flair, traded for grit in the field. This picture shows him at Big Bend. Courtesy DeGolyer Library, Southern Methodist University, Dallas, Texas.

volcanic eruption of Mount Pelée and the total destruction of the town of Saint Pierre on the Caribbean island of Martinique. He conducted his studies of Caribbean islands under the auspices of Alexander Agassiz of Harvard University, with whom he also had a falling out.

But Robert T. Hill was a survivor and a person of tremendous pride. He was an excellent rock man, so he was always able to fall back on his abilities as a petroleum geologist. In his later years he became a columnist for the *Dallas Morning News*, writing about a number of topics ranging from politics to life in the old days. "Musings and Mutterings," he called his column.

His studies of the sequence of rocks and fossils in Central Texas were phenomenal. They remain the basis for our understanding of the physical relationships of these rocks even today. It was while conducting those studies in 1886 that Hill examined the rock strata along the Texas Pacific Railroad tracks between Elmo in Kaufman County and Millsap in Parker County west of Fort Worth. He found dinosaur bones along the Lick Branch of Grindstone Creek, most likely near Lambert Switch, just a bit east of Millsap. A highway runs past there today. These may or may not have been the first dinosaurs Hill found, but now he was a professional.

Hill had the bones identified by the legendary Edward Drinker Cope, naturalist extraordinaire, held in such high regard by some that his skull was preserved after his death at the University of Pennsylvania in Philadelphia. It is still there. Whatever the quality of Cope's scientific reputation, the dinosaur bones from Texas identified by him have now been lost. I have never been able to find a reference to them in the great paleontologist's publications, nor did Cope mention them in his letters to Hill. Since the ignominious identification and subsequent loss of Hill's bones, the dinosaurs of Central Texas have been neither forgotten nor ignored, but they have not been exactly front-burner items, either. Their full importance is only just now coming to light. That makes them all the more exciting.

Hill did not spend all of his time in Central Texas. He also headed west, where he floated down the Rio Grande to conduct a reconnaissance survey along the cliffs of the Big Bend country. It was a land of outlaws and tough hombres back then. His guide was Jim MacMahon, said to be the ugliest man in Texas. He was ugly even as a child, the story goes: so ugly his mother had to be tied to her bed so that he could nurse!

Dinosaur remains occur in quantity in the Big Bend, but Hill did not find any. That came later. J. A. Udden made the first collections. In Udden's 1907 report on the geology of the Big Bend, he included a letter from Samuel Wendell Williston of the University of Chicago, to whom he had sent the bones. Williston identified at least three different species of dinosaurs that he said were new to science, as well as a turtle and a crocodile. Even so, the discovery did not seem to generate much interest. The great quantities of bone at Big Bend only began to attract the attention they deserved in 1936 with the work of Ross A. Maxwell, a geologist for the National Park Service and the first superintendent of Big Bend National Park. Paleontologists from the University of Oklahoma began to take interest in bones found by workers in the Civilian Conservation Corps and others who were developing a state park in the Chisos Mountains and environs. These bones were assembled and placed in a museum housed in a wood-frame barracks located in what is now called the Basin, high within the Chisos. On Christmas Eve, 1941, a fire destroyed the building and its contents. Inside were the bones of duck-billed hadrosaurs and horned ceratopsian dinosaurs.

In the late 1930s, William S. Strain, a student from Oklahoma, took a job at the Texas College of Mines and Metallurgy—now the University of Texas at El Paso—and began a program to collect dinosaurs through the WPA. Substantial collections were made, but not all the specimens have been studied, even today. Strain's success spurred J. Willis Stoval of the University of

The museum—a converted barracks—in the Basin, high in the Chisos Mountains of Big Bend, which housed dinosaur bones until it burned down on Christmas Eve, 1941. Courtesy of Wann Langston, Jr.

Oklahoma to send three more students—Wann Langston, Jr., Donald E. Savage, and William N. McAnulty—down to collect in 1938.

Barnum Brown, the American Museum paleontologist to whom Roland T. Bird was to ship the Glen Rose footprints, entered the Big Bend scene about this time. Brown had received a letter from a Big Bend rancher reporting some fossils. He followed up the lead through an avocational collector, Don Guadagni, who sent Brown a large fossil palm leaf. The next year Brown sent Erich M. Schlaikjer from Brooklyn College and William O. Sweet to West Texas. Schlaikjer and Sweet collected sauropod and horned dinosaur bones and sent them back to the museum in New York.

Brown thus had two fossil-collecting teams active in Texas: one led by Bird at Glen Rose, and the other led by Schlaikjer in the Big Bend. His interest piqued, in 1940 Brown flew to Dallas, where Bird picked him up at the airport and whisked him to Glen Rose to see the trackways. Erich Schlaikjer joined them at the Paluxy River (which explains how a Texas footprint ended up at Brooklyn College, where Schlaikjer taught).

After being awed by the sauropod tracks, Brown and Schlaikjer headed for the Big Bend country. It was mid-July. Toward the end of August, smack in the middle of the hottest part of the year, Schlaikjer had to return to his teaching. Barnum Brown needed help and did not drive, so Bird completed the collection of the sauropod trackway at Glen Rose and headed for Marathon to work with Brown in Big Bend. Although Brown was getting on in years and Bird's health was less than good, the two paleontological greats braved the hardships and heat of the Texas desert, found dinosaurs, dug them out, and shipped them back to New York. One of the bones they collected— a huge neck vertebra of the sauropod *Alamosaurus* (AL-uh-moh-SAWR-us)—

Wann Langston, Jr., (in pith helmet, his trademark for the time) with William N. McAnulty excavating a hadrosaur in Big Bend in the late 1930s. Photograph by Donald E. Savage.

A Works Progress Administration fossil excavation crew in Big Bend during the late 1930s. Courtesy of Wann Langston, Jr.

was the last dinosaur bone that Barnum Brown, who began his dinosaur hunting for the American Museum in 1897, ever collected for that institution.

The area surrounding Amarillo, Lubbock, and Big Spring in the Panhandle is the third major area in Texas that yields dinosaur remains. It is a dry, dusty spread, the southern extent of the Great Plains. It stands as a flat table, the Llano Estacado, high above the surrounding countryside. Ancient Indians scraped shallow wells through its parched surface, drawing water to slake their thirst. The Indians of the 1870s dug wells—rather than frequent known springs—so as not to be ambushed by the army.

The rugged slopes that lead up to the Llano Estacado are a bulwark. They appear as protecting ramparts to the tableland when approached from a distance. The ramparts ring the Llano from the Canadian River in the north to Big Spring in the south. Eons of erosion on the Llano escarpment have cut canyons and sculpted the soft rocks into stark and barren badlands, naked and exposed, without a dense and protective covering of plants. Lots of fossils can be found in those exposures. Most of them are from the Age of Mammals and much younger than the dinosaurs. But in several long stretches, red rocks are exposed in the escarpment: that is where the oldest Texas dinosaurs can be found.

In 1892, our old friend Edward Drinker Cope made his second trip to Texas. He went first to Dallas, where he met up with W. F. Cummins, the geologist for northern Texas of the Texas Geological Survey. Then it was off to Big Spring to explore the Llano Estacado for fossils. Cummins had been there before. This time the party numbered six in all, including Cummins's eighteen-year-old son, Duncan, who ran off after a couple of weeks. He supposedly headed back to Big Spring, 125 miles distant, without money or blankets. I do not know whatever became of Duncan. His father was a longtime collector for Cope, particularly in the older rocks near Wichita Falls. The fossils Cummins found that were studied by Cope are now mostly at the University of Texas at Austin, but there is also a smattering that found their way back East.

Following Cummins and Cope, E. C. Case and his students from the University of Michigan amassed a large suite of fossils from the red beds of the Llano escarpment in the early part of this century. One of the students was John A. Wilson, who first worked the Texas Panhandle with Case in 1934.

Not long after that, a new phase began. During the late 1930s, about the same time the WPA was working in Big Bend and on the Paluxy River tracks, other WPA crews excavated around the Llano Estacado, notably in Palo Duro Canyon. A major WPA program was established at West Texas State Teachers' College (now West Texas A&M University) in Canyon, run by C. Stuart Johnston. He opened excavations in twenty-six Panhandle counties. His doctoral studies focused on fossil mammals of the Panhandle, much younger than the dinosaurs, and extensive collections of them were made under his direction.

Johnston was a dapper fellow with a thin pencil mustache. Old photographs show him dressed neatly for the field. Johnston was fresh from the University of Oklahoma, where he was working toward his doctorate under J. Willis Stoval. As a young geology professor, he was inspiring to students. One of them, Donald E. Savage, was led into a long and successful paleontological career because of Johnston's enthusiasm and influence.

Johnston died suddenly on July 24, 1939, on a trip to Cambridge, where, under unexplained circumstances, he was found dead in a Boston hotel room. After his death, the field operations were taken over for a while by his wife, Margaret. She worked in the older rocks, digging up the contemporaries of early dinosaurs. Important collections were made under her direction in the vicinity of the Herring Ranch at pleasant-sounding Rotten Hill and at other places in Potter County near Amarillo. Mrs. Johnston's fieldwork ended in 1941. What a job the Johnstons had done in just a few short years in the field. The collections made under their direction are extraordinary and contain many interesting examples of life as it was when dinosaurs had not yet become dominant. The collection is still in Canyon, at the university, in the Panhandle-Plains Museum.

In Howard County near Big Spring, Grayson Meade of the University of Texas supervised the WPA crews working the Otis Chalk area. Glen Evans—the guy who accompanied Bird to the dinosaur trackways at Glen Rose—was also a Panhandle supervisor. Joseph T. Gregory worked in the paleontology laboratory in Austin, where the results of the fieldwork were shipped. It was a beehive of paleontological activity, with as many as fifty people carefully extracting bones from the plaster and burlap casts that jacketed the fossils to protect them while being transported from the excavations to the laboratory in town.

Some of the paleontologists who worked the dinosaur beds of Texas in the 1930s and '40s went on to assume commanding roles in their profession. After the Second World War, Joe Gregory took a position at Yale, returning

Margaret Johnston shown (probably) at Rotten Hill in the Panhandle. After the untimely death of her husband in 1939, Margaret became one of the first women to direct field crews in paleontology. Courtesy Panhandle-Plains Museum, Canyon, Texas.

to the Panhandle to conduct his own fieldwork. He and Don Savage are now retired from the University of California at Berkeley. Jack Wilson spent most of his career as a professor at the University of Texas, retiring a few years ago. Grayson Meade went off to teach at Texas Tech. Glen Evans stayed at the University of Texas. Then, in the 1950s, after more than a decade of the finest fossiling in the state, both Evans and Meade left academia for the oil patch. Fast friends forever, they never lost their love of fossils or their reputations for quality work and in-depth knowledge—not just about fossils, but about things geological and archaeological as well. They never lost their happy enthusiasm, either. You should hear their voices bubble over with the spirit that exudes from the salt of the Texas earth.

One of the students who went to Big Bend from Oklahoma in 1938 was Wann Langston, Jr. Langston, more than any of the others, stuck with Texas dinosaurs. Nowadays he is a still active but retired professor from the University of Texas. He is unquestionably the patriarch of Texas dinosaur paleontologists, having five decades of field and research experience with the dinosaurs of this state, their bones, and their footprints. Langston is the textbook example of a dedicated, exacting paleontologist. Through his teaching, his graduate students and colleagues have a link with the heady times when Texas dinosaur paleontology was in its infancy.

Now it seems that Texas has its fair share of dinosaur paleontologists. At the University of Texas, Timothy Rowe has stepped into Langston's shoes and brought his high-powered computer skills to the job. Jeff Pittman, a student of Langston and an expert on dinosaur footprints, now teaches at East Texas State University. Dawn Adams, who studies how dinosaurs move, is at Baylor. Sankar Chatterjee, at Texas Tech, has announced startling discoveries from the Panhandle recently. Thomas Lehman, also at Texas Tech and a former student of Langston, is best known for his studies of horned dinosaurs and the geological context in which they are found. Tarleton State University's Phillip Murry is an expert on Panhandle fossils—he studied them for his doctoral dissertation—plus a lot more. Dale Winkler, associate director of the Shuler Museum of Paleontology at Southern Methodist University (where I teach), studies dinosaur evolutionary relationships, their growth from hatchling to adult, and their ecology. Phil, Dale, and I have been working together for the past decade trying to understand more fully the dinosaurs from the heart of Texas.

With so much dinosaur talent scattered around the state, it is little wonder that the story of Texas dinosaurs is coming to light in detail never before possible. That story is also becoming more accessible to the public at large through the displays and educational programs of museums like the Fort Worth

Museum of Science and History, the Dallas Museum of Natural History, the Panhandle-Plains Museum in Canyon, and the Houston Museum of Natural Science. Each in its own special way welcomes dinosaur lovers of all ages. Of these fine institutions, only the Houston museum has a professional paleontologist, Christopher Cunningham, on staff. However, all of them realize the educational, entertainment, and excitement value of dinosaurs, especially those found right here in our own state. Of course, with so much research activity focusing on dinosaurs, our understanding of these magnificent creatures and their habitats must be continually revised. The story is never complete—or completely correct—for very long.

So what is it that is so special about Texas dinosaurs, besides the fact that they are found in this state? What is so interesting about them?

I think there are three fundamental aspects of Texas dinosaurs that make them both interesting and significant well beyond the borders of this state. Their significance is general and applicable all over the world because that is what studies of dinosaurs tell us about: the world as a whole. They tell us how it has changed through millions of years of geologic time. What is profound about that statement is that if those specific changes had not occurred in the way they did in the past, the world would not be as it is now. We would probably not even be here. Maybe some other species would dominate in our place. Maybe it would have been a dinosaur. We are truly a product of history.

So how has this large, irregular spot on the globe, currently called Texas, changed through time? What was it like in the geological past? How does its history fit in with that of the rest of the world? The three aspects of Texas dinosaurs that allow us to address those questions are the diversity, the age, and the geography of Texas dinosaurs in its broadest context. There are currently over three hundred different and distinct species of dinosaurs known worldwide. That number can be expected to grow because discoveries of new dinosaurs are made fairly regularly, especially in such places as South America and China, but also in Texas.

The best way to make sense out of all these species and to understand the diversity of Texas dinosaurs is to place each onto an evolutionary tree. Evolutionary trees are diagrams that show the relationship of one species to another. Trees represent an organization because twigs join into branches, which join the trunk. Each twig, or in this case each species, becomes grouped with others. At some level, all share a common trunk.

There are many kinds of paleontological trees used to group fossil species. It is important to recognize that an ancestral species will pass on its unique features through its genes only to its descendants. Its descendants, therefore, form a special group—or branch, if you will—because they are all descended from a common ancestor. Of course, even ancestors have ancestors; that is to say, they relate back to larger branches. Just as there are twigs, branches, bigger branches, and trunks in a tree, with every twig fitting somewhere in the hierarchy and belonging to many larger and more inclusive groups, so, too, do evolutionary trees rank and group species.

In the fossils that concern us, the characteristic features passed on by an ancestor may be seen in the skeleton. Depending on how far back down the tree the common ancestor is and on the particular features passed on to descendants, the groups will be more or less inclusive. That is how the systematic pattern of relationships among dinosaurs is puzzled out: groups within groups, all based on common ancestry, whether more or less distant; all defined by features seen in the fossils.

Although dinosaurs are generally thought of as giants, large size is not a defining characteristic of the group as a whole. That is because even though many species are of large size, not all of them are. The earliest known dinosaurs are small, although soon after the evolutionary origin of dinosaurs larger species begin to appear in the rock record. Those from the middle and later portions of the dinosaur era generally are larger; the largest known species lived in the middle of the Age of Reptiles (more about the chronology of dinosaurs later). However, even some of the latest species are tiny compared to the common perception of dinosaurs.

With only a few arguable exceptions, dinosaurs can be divided into two fundamental groups regardless of size. The exceptions are the earliest known dinosaur species, which appear to be primitive, lacking the anatomical sophistication observed in the rest of the dinosaurs. The primary groups, excluding those few archaic species that may not fit, are the lizard-hipped, or saurischian (sore-ISS-kee-an), dinosaurs and the bird-hipped, or ornithischian (orn-ith-ISS-kee-an), dinosaurs. As reflected by the names, the differences are best observed in the pelvic girdles; that is, in the bones where the hind legs attach. The names also seem to imply that one group of dinosaurs has hips like lizards whereas the other has hips like birds. That is only superficially so, and in a way that has no real meaning, as we will see later on. The names may be strange, but the two groups are realistic and certainly useful for understanding dinosaur relationships. Both ornithischian and saurischian dinosaurs are found in Texas.

Dinosaurs as a whole are basically and primitively bipedal, which means they walked about on their hind legs. The earliest dinosaurs were that way. Dinosaurian pelvic girdles were functionally related to the ability to walk upright. The differences between saurischian and ornithischian hips reflect alternatives in the way bony support and muscle attachments evolved and in the way that these facilitated movement and posture. One result of bipedality is the freeing of the hands and arms from quadrupedal locomotion. They can do other things. That happened in human evolution, so now I can type these words (albeit with only two fingers). Dinosaurs never reached that point. While their thumbs were somewhat opposable, they were short, as were their little fingers. In *Iguanodon* (i-GUAN-uh-don), the second dinosaur ever described, the thumb was a spike. The original reconstructions mistakenly placed the thumb spike on the tip of the nose like a horn. Some species lacked thumbs and little fingers altogether. *Tyrannosaurus rex* (tye-RAN-uh-SAWR-us RECKS) reduced the number of fingers to two. In yet other species, especially those that were very large, the method of locomotion reverted from two feet back to four again, and the hands were modified accordingly.

Saurischian dinosaurs include both the biggest and the baddest dinosaurian species. *T. rex* is a saurischian and so is *Diplodocus* (di-pluh-DOH-kus). These two exemplify the two main groups of lizard-hipped dinosaurs. *T. rex* and all the other predatory meat eaters are termed theropods and moved about on their hind legs. *T. rex* is the most famous, but there are many other species of theropods, most of which cannot compare with *T. rex* in size and many that do not look all that similar to it. Some ostrich-mimic dinosaurs, for instance, lacked teeth and look a bit like the birds from whom they take their common name.

The sauropodomorphs are the second group of lizard-hipped dinosaurs. This group includes the largest animals ever to walk the Earth. It includes brontosaurs such as *Apatosaurus* and *Diplodocus*. The weights of these animals reached into the tens of tons. The largest estimates approach an unlikely one hundred tons. Even so, sauropodomorphs attained huge size by any measure. Because they were so heavy, their straight legs were positioned directly under their bodies, as in elephants, in the fashion called graviportal. The longest sauropodomorph—and the longest dinosaur of all—is *Seismosaurus* (SYZE-muh-SAWR-us), estimated to be as long as half a football field. Sauropodomorphs became quadrupedal, probably along with the attainment of large and ultimately gigantic size. All were plant eaters. The heads of the sauropod giants, perched at the end of long necks, seem grotesquely small for their bodies. Symmetry with the neck is provided by a long tail. In some sauropodomorphs the tail tapers down to a long, thin end, reminiscent of a whiplash. In others, it is more blunt. Strangely, one family of sauropodomorphs has bony armor in the skin. Within the sauropodomorphs, two groups can be recognized: the generally older and smaller prosauropods, and the giants and their close kin, which are simply referred to as sauropods. Prosauropods are questionably noted in Texas, but sauropods definitely are. Like the

Saurischian
(lizard-hipped)

Theropods

Sauropods

There are two fundamental groups of dinosaurs: lizard-hipped or saurischian, shown on the left, and bird-hipped or ornithischian, on the right. Texas has representatives of all the major groups of both lizard-hipped and bird-hipped dinosaurs. Illustration by Karen Carr.

sauropodomorphs, the theropods, the other big group of lizard-hipped dinosaurs, are also found in Texas.

The bird-hipped dinosaurs, or ornithischians, exhibit an extremely broad range of body forms. Again, as in the saurischians, there are both bipedal and quadrupedal species. The distinction may make little difference for some ornithischians, because pivoting at the hip may have allowed them to locomote either bipedally or quadrupedally as necessary. Many older reconstructions display some ornithischians as bipedal, while now those same species are known to be quadrupedal. That is progress. At any rate, there are both bipedal and quadrupedal species of bird-hipped dinosaurs. All ornithischians were herbivores.

Ornithischian
(Bird-hipped)

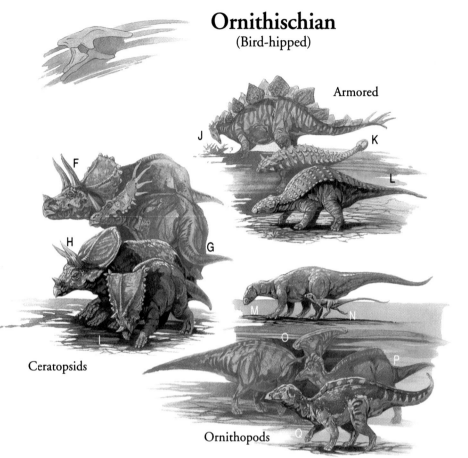

Armored

Ceratopsids

Ornithopods

Ornithischian diversity is divided among three groups. The first of these is the ornithopod group. The word *ornithopod* means "bird foot." The more primitive ornithopods are bipedal and small, while the more derived forms are larger. Their hands have been modified into hooves, indicating that they proceeded on all fours. Primitively, the teeth of ornithopods are simple and leaf-shaped, placed along the jaw in a single row. Early on in ornithopod evolution, the front teeth were lost: primitive species have them, advanced species do not. The front of the jaws was broad, in some species quite flattened, and covered with a horny bill. Because of this, these ornithischians are known as the duck-billed dinosaurs. Advanced ornithopods also evolved batteries of hundreds of small teeth that worked as a unit along the jawbones at the sides of the mouth. Worn-out teeth were constantly replaced by new ones, thereby maintaining a sharp cutting edge for chopping vegetation. Ornithopods had cheeks, which held the food in their mouths while it was being cropped and masticated. Many later ornithopod species were very large—although never as large as the gigantic sauropods—and developed ornate bony crests on their skulls for display or vocalization or both. The sounds resonating through the nasal crests of these large ornithopods were low and mournful—and difficult for a predator to track.

The second group of bird-hipped dinosaurs comprises the armored dinosaurs. All of them were quadrupedal, their heads were held low, and their teeth were simple and leaf-shaped. They were herbivores that most likely fed off plants growing close to the ground.

The armored dinosaurs can be further divided. Stegosaurs are the dinosaurs with bony plates running in staggered or parallel rows down the center of the back. At the end of the tail, and in some species in the shoulder region, long pointed spikes provided protection. The second group of armored dinosaurs includes both ankylosaurids and nodosaurids. Both had skulls encrusted and overgrown with bony armor plates developed from the skin. The rest of the body was covered with a mail of dermal bones, giving these dinosaurs the appearance of animated tanks. Ankylosaurids had a bony club at the end of the tail while nodosaurids did not.

The third big division of ornithischians includes the horned dinosaurs like *Triceratops* (try-SER-uh-tops) and their relatives, the boneheads or pachycephalosaurs. These were all plant eaters. The horned dinosaurs, or ceratopsians, even developed a dental battery similar to that of advanced ornithopods. The boneheads were bipedal. They developed greatly thickened domes of bone on top of the head, surrounded below by knobby excrescences, giving them a strange, bald-headed appearance. The ceratopsians, on the other hand, were large quadrupeds. The biggest skulls in the dinosaur world are found on the ceratopsians, taking up as much as a third of the total body length. The back of the head flared out into a large bony shield or frill. Horns for defense and intraspecific rituals resided at various places on the skull, depending on the species. In *Triceratops* they are over the eyes, on the brow, and on the nose. *Pentaceratops* (PEN-tuh-SER-uh-tops), as another example, has horns similar to *Triceratops* but with smaller ones developed in the cheek region as well. Most ceratopsians had no front teeth. The huge, broad skull tapers down to a point toward the nose, and the mouth ends in a narrow, toothless beak. Representatives of all the major groups have been found in Texas.

Texas cannot brag that it sports all of the more than three hundred species of dinosaurs known in the world—no place can. As shown in the discussion above, however, Texas has representatives of all of the basic groups of dinosaurs. Such diversity in this one Texas-size region is remarkable, because it samples nearly the entire range of dinosaurian evolution. That, right away, gives us a clue that we must be dealing with a large expanse of time because dinosaur species, in their fantastic array of diversity, are not all to be found within a single short time interval. In fact, the three areas within Texas that yield dinosaur treasures are of different ages. Dinosaur-bearing deposits in the Panhandle are the oldest, dating back well over 200 million years to the beginning of the Age of Reptiles, or Mesozoic Era, as it is more properly known. In Central Texas, the dinosaurs range in age from a bit older than 100 million years to a bit younger than that. Big Bend has the youngest of all the Texas dinosaurs, dating right to the big extinction at the end of the Mesozoic, 66 million years ago.

Part of the diversity of Texas dinosaurs can be explained by realizing that Texas rocks sample portions of the entire extent of the dinosaurs' reign on Earth. The older part of the Mesozoic has different species from the middle, which again has different species from the end. The differences in species are manifested in the restructuring of ecological communities through time as environmental conditions change. This is related to the way species evolve through natural selection.

The ornithischians and saurischians appear early in the Mesozoic as a basic dichotomy—two branches on the dinosaur family tree—that developed soon after the origin of dinosaurs. After that, the subordinate groups (the smaller branches and twigs, as it were) developed and evolved through time. These groups were all influenced by the other members of their communities, both plant and animal, and by the physical conditions under which they lived. To appreciate that fully, we must take a closer look at geologic time, the recognition of which is one of the great achievements of the human intellect.

All around us are clues to the antiquity of the Earth, if we are aware of what they mean. One very simple and basic line of evidence is the way that sedimentary rocks are laid down in layers. If you think about it, common sense says that the layer on the bottom of a stack of strata must be older than the layers that lie on top of it. That is the principle of superposition, and it is the foundation on which the geologic time scale was based. It follows logically that if the layers of stacked sedimentary rock contain fossils, those fossils in the lowest layer must be older than any fossils that occur in the layers above. And because fossils are different from layer to layer going up the rock column, that tells us that the species of life that inhabit the Earth have changed through time. There is no question about that. Otherwise, we would expect to see *T. rex* or *Diplodocus* or some other denizen of deep time around every corner. Obviously, we do not.

Fossils extracted from rocks deposited in specific time intervals of the geologic past tend to be characteristic of that particular time and different from the times that precede or follow. Therefore, if we find fossils in one place that are similar to those in another, we infer that the rocks entombing them are of similar age. Now of course, most fossils are discovered on or near the surface of the ground, where they have been exposed by the processes of erosion. Moreover, no place on Earth has a complete section of rock recording every layer ever deposited throughout all of geologic time. But because we can use fossils to correlate ages of rocks from place to place, we can certainly build a composite sequence of the history of life based on fossils. That is what was done by early researchers of Earth history to develop a geologic time scale. Major changes in life inhabiting the Earth—such as extinction events when many species died out, sometimes suddenly—marked the boundaries of geologic units that help us to tell geologic time.

The big divisions of the geologic time scale that encompass the span of vertebrate animals are the Paleozoic Era, or Age of Ancient Life (Age of Fishes); the Mesozoic Era, or Age of Middle Life (Age of Reptiles); and Cenozoic Era, or Age of Modern Life (Age of Mammals). The Mesozoic is composed of three parts: from oldest to youngest, the Triassic, Jurassic, and Cretaceous periods. Dinosaurs have their origin in the Triassic. The extinction that brought about their demise marks the end of the Cretaceous.

Preceding the Paleozoic is an even longer interval of time. That time interval, which encompasses most of Earth history, is called the Precambrian. At its beginning fossils are absent, although they soon begin to turn up, albeit diminutive and rare. It is only with the beginning of the Paleozoic Era, continuing up toward the present, that fossils become abundant—so abundant that their succession became the basis of the geologic time scale.

It is curious that the Paleozoic is known as the *Age of Fishes* when there are still fish around today. Use of the term Age of Fishes does not mean that fish are limited to that era. It simply means that fishes were the dominant vertebrates for most of that time. Certain kinds of fishes, in the broad sense, are characteristic of it. None of those species still exists, but evolution has brought their much-modified relatives up to the present. Dinosaurs did not exist during the Paleozoic, although other reptiles did. By the beginning of the Cenozoic, dinosaurs, as we usually think of them, were all gone.

Now we know from superposition how to determine which fossil is older than what and how the words of the geologic time scale were derived. We also know where the dinosaurs fit into this scale. But all of that does not tell us what we really want to know: how old are the fossils in numbers of years? How can we find out?

The techniques of determining absolute geologic age are familiar enough to most people that, when asked how to find out how old a dinosaur is, the response might very well be an enthusiastic, "Radiocarbon dating." That response would merit an equally enthusiastic, "Wrong!" But there is conceptual merit to it.

Radiocarbon dating works by determining the amount of radioactive carbon in a sample and comparing that to the amounts of elements present that are not radioactive. Because radioactive decay transforms one sort of atom into another, the amount of radioactive parent element in a good sample will always become less and less through time as it decays. The rate of decay varies from element to element. Radioactive carbon decays very rapidly. For that reason, radiocarbon dating is only good for dating samples that are no more than about seventy thousand years old at the most. The mass extinction of dinosaurs occurred at least sixty-six million years ago, so obviously radiocarbon dating cannot be used with dinosaurs. Another radioactive element must be chosen, one with a slower rate of decay.

If radioactive carbon decays so rapidly, you might ask where it comes from. Why isn't it all decayed away? The answer is that radioactive carbon is formed in the atmosphere by the bombardment of nitrogen with cosmic rays. (Neat, huh?) Because radioactive carbon reacts chemically just like normal, everyday nonradioactive carbon, it combines with oxygen to form carbon dioxide, which is taken up by plants during photosynthesis to build sugar and starch. That means radioactive carbon is actually incorporated into the bodies of living organisms: either in the plants that take up carbon dioxide from the atmosphere or by animals in the food chain that eat the plants containing radioactive carbon. That, in turn, means that after an organism dies, no more radioactive carbon is incorporated into the body. As the radioactive carbon decays, the amount that is there diminishes. An age can be determined because we know precisely how fast radioactive carbon decays, and that rate never varies. Radiocarbon dating can be performed on samples of the fossil that contain radioactive carbon; that is, if it is not so old geologically that not enough radioactive carbon is left to date.

None of that matters in examining dinosaurs because they are not geologically young enough for radiocarbon dating to be used. The radioactive elements used to date dinosaurs, like radioactive potassium, decay much more slowly. Such radioactive elements are not produced in the atmosphere but occur as natural constituents of some rocks. Moreover, these elements used to date dinosaur bones are not found in the fossils per se. They are found in crystals that are a part of the rocks and strata that comprise the geological section in which the fossils are found. So the dates date the rocks and the rocks limit the age of the fossils. If a radiometric date is determined on a crystal taken from a layer above a dinosaur bone, the bone can be no younger geologically than that date. It must be older because of superposition. The fossil is from a stratum that lies below the layer with the dated crystal. If there is also a date from a stratum below the bone, the bone has to be younger than it is. Thus, the fossil's age is bracketed by radiometric dates.

In compiling an accurate and meaningful record of geologic time, it must be remembered that not all rocks have fossils in them and not all rocks have the right mineral composition or history to yield reliable radiometric dates. Therefore, both radiometric dating and the geological sequence of fossils, plus some other techniques I have not mentioned, are used to build a reliable chronology. As such, geological dating is continually being revised and updated as it is tested by new dates, new fossils, and new observations that do not fit well with established views. That is a sign of an exciting, viable, and interesting science. Nevertheless, the broad framework of the geologic time scale and its calibration with radiometric dates has attained a relative degree of stability. The result is that we can discuss the ages of Texas dinosaurs in reasonable and accurate terms based on the global knowledge of geologic time.

We know, for instance, that the dinosaurs from the Panhandle date back to the Triassic, the oldest of the three periods in the Mesozoic. The Triassic began 245 million years ago and lasted for 37 million years. It ended by 208 million years ago. The Panhandle dinosaurs are Late Triassic in age, well over 200 million years old, dating back to very near the time that dinosaurs are thought to have evolved.

The second division of the Mesozoic Era is the Jurassic Period. That is the time represented by the bones at Dinosaur National Monument in Utah. It began when the Triassic ended (208 million years ago) and lasted some 64 million years until 144 million years ago. It is characterized by an abundance of giants like *Diplodocus, Apatosaurus,* and *Seismosaurus.* It is also the time of *Stegosaurus* (STEG-uh-SAWR-us) and *Allosaurus.* There are no Jurassic dinosaurs known from Texas, but they occur just to the north in the panhandle of Oklahoma and to the west in New Mexico.

The third and youngest division of the Mesozoic Era is the Cretaceous Period. The Cretaceous extends from 144 million to about 66 million years ago, a duration of roughly 80 million years—nearly half of the total time of the Mesozoic when dinosaurs ruled the Earth. The Cretaceous is officially divided into two parts, Early and Late. The boundary lies at 97.5 million years ago. It so happens that dinosaurs of the Early Cretaceous just before the boundary and those of the Late Cretaceous just after it are particularly poorly known or understood. There are big differences in the species of dinosaurs that occur on either side of this boundary. The rocks of Central Texas straddle the Early Cretaceous–Late Cretaceous boundary, and therefore, they provide a good place to study the transition in land-dwelling faunas. What is more, there are only a few places where the transition can be studied, making the Central Texas rocks all the more important scientifically. The end of the Cretaceous—and the end of the Mesozoic, for that matter—is recorded in the rocks of the Big Bend, recognized by the extinction of dinosaurs.

So you see, not only do we have a great diversity of saurischian and ornithischian dinosaur species found in Texas, they are scattered across nearly the entire Mesozoic history of dinosaurs, from close to the time of dinosaur origins up to the big extinction. Although there are no Jurassic dinosaurs known from Texas, their occurrence near the Early Cretaceous–Late Cretaceous boundary in the middle portion of the Mesozoic helps document the important faunal transition in life on land at that time. Big Bend dinosaurs take us up to the end.

To place all this dinosaur time talk in perspective, dinosaurs lived in the Mesozoic Era from 230 to 66 million years ago, a duration of some 164 million years. The Cenozoic, or Age of Mammals, in which we now live has been going on for a mere 66 million years—nearly 100 million years shorter than the Mesozoic reign of the dinosaurs. To be sure, the species of dinosaurs evolved and changed throughout the Mesozoic with no single species lasting the whole time. But the same is true for the Cenozoic as well. No species of mammal has existed throughout the entire Cenozoic. The human family, for example, as a group of upright walking primates, has been around for 3.7 million years; our closest relatives for about a million and a half; and our species for well under a million years. You might be surprised to know that a fundamental trunk of the mammalian tree originated at about the same time dinosaurs did, over 200 million years ago. However, for most of the past 200 million years, mammals have been diminutive and inconsequential as authority figures. Only after the massive extinction of dinosaurs 66 million years ago did mammals conquer the Earth.

In scientific parlance, a species is a group of organisms that can interbreed and produce living offspring that can also reproduce. With fossils, you cannot devise mating experiments to see who can mate with whom to produce fertile young. For most living species that has not been done either. Usually, a group of fossils that share a close similarity in shape, form, size, and structure is recognized as a species. In our living world today, individuals belonging to a single species are more similar to each other than to members of a different species. In other words, members of the same species look alike. The procedure used in defining fossil species relies on that concept. Species more closely related to each other than to anything else are placed in the same genus. Viewed as an evolutionary tree, a species is the terminal twig; a genus is the stem by which several species are joined. A scientific name is a binomial comprising the generic and specific epithets, as in *Tyrannosaurus rex. Tyrannosaurus* is the generic name, *rex* is the specific name.

It has been estimated that dinosaur genera existed on Earth a bit less than 8 million years on average. That is comparable to how long mammalian genera stick around. So the thing about comparing dinosaurs and mammals is not that any particular species or genus endured for such a long time. Rather, it is that the dinosaurs as a group did not just exist but ruled the Earth as the dominant group of land-dwelling vertebrates for so long, especially compared to mammals. On that score, we mammals have 100 million years of catching up to do to be the masters of the planet for as long as dinosaurs were—if we can last that long without irreconcilably fouling our Earth nest.

There is one other point to be made in comparing the duration of dinosaurs with that of mammals. As stated above, both dinosaurs and mammals had their origins in the Triassic Period. Dinosaurs then took over the terrestrial world while mammals remained obscure in their shadows and footsteps. It was only after the dominating dinosaurs of the Mesozoic became extinct that mammals truly blossomed and radiated in exuberant diversity during the Cenozoic. Mammals became the epitome of animal life on land while it appears that dinosaurs were banished to the rubbish heap of Earth history.

Nothing could be further from the truth. Although dinosaurs in the classic sense of *T. rex* and *Triceratops* did die out at the end of the Cretaceous Period, one very likely dinosaur scion—one twig of the tree that sprouted early in dinosaur history—did not go extinct. It grew into a branch and lives on even today: it is the birds. If that is true, then we can think of birds as the feathery, fluttery dinosaurs that they are. If we do, we see that dinosaurs remain even today a remarkably successful and diverse group of animals, rulers of the skies if not of the land. We can say that not only did dinosaurs and mammals evolve at about the same time, but they exist together now. And they have done so all through the Age of Reptiles and the Age of Mammals.

Recognizing birds as dinosaurs makes them both more interesting. There is still a great deal we want to know about the giants, the traditional dinosaurs that brought fame to the group. The focus remains on the Mesozoic denizens, although we will return briefly to the subject of birds as dinosaurs later on.

During all the time of the Mesozoic (and since), the Earth has not stood still. It never has. It is a dynamic planet with internal forces and mechanisms

that drive large-scale processes on the surface. One of the manifestations of those processes is the phenomenon called continental drift. What that means is that the positions of continents, no matter how big and stable they may seem, are not fixed. The continents move, changing latitude and longitude through geologic time in a complex interplay of geometry and geography. Continents drift because of a process called plate tectonics, which simply means that the Earth's exterior surface is composed of huge, rigid segments called plates. These plates move relative to each other; they move and slide and push and pull against each other. If one moves, the others must compensate in some way. Otherwise, the Earth would be growing or shrinking or otherwise deforming in ways that we know it is not doing. The real manifestations of plate movements that we can feel and see most clearly are earthquakes, volcanoes, and mountains.

The Earth quakes when plates move. The movement occurs along breaks in the rocks of the Earth's crust, called faults. Faults are concentrated at plate boundaries, like, for example, the San Andreas fault in California, although others are found away from the margins. In Texas we have the relatively inactive Balcones fault zone, extending from Austin toward Dallas. There are also many faults in the mountains of West Texas.

Mountains and volcanoes are formed when plates collide and one rides over another, and where plates are spreading apart. In the first case, the rock that makes up a plate is consumed as one plate slides underneath another and is incorporated into the Earth's interior. The sliding of the subducting plate

LEGEND:

A. Volcanoes;
B. Rising Magma;
C. Subduction Zone;
D. New Ocean Crust Forming;
E. Continent

Continents drift because the plates on which they ride move relative to each other, converging and forming mountains where they collide, or forming oceans where they diverge as molten rock wells up.
Illustration by Karen Carr.

beneath the overriding plate generates tremendous amounts of heat energy through the friction of their movements. In the second case, where plates are spreading apart, the plates enlarge at their margins where new rock is added, carried up as molten lava from the depths of the Earth. As the plate grows larger along its newly formed edge, it is consumed by subduction at the opposite margin. The leading edge being subducted into the Earth pulls the plate along behind it while upwelling molten rock pushes from the spreading edge. At both boundaries, heat is carried to the surface from deep in the Earth by volcanoes.

The heat and molten rock escaping from within the Earth form volcanic mountains. Some of the greatest suites of volcanic mountains lie in long chains that bisect the ocean floor, huge in stature but nonetheless largely concealed by seawater. An example is the mid-Atlantic ridge, which runs down the center of the Atlantic. Islands are found where it cuts the surface. Iceland, with its volcanoes and hot springs, is an example of an island on the mid-Atlantic ridge. These undersea mountain chains lie at the juncture of two plates. A plate enlarges along these volcanic chains by the extrusion of lava, the newly formed rock pushing older plate rock away in opposite directions from the ridge. While that is happening at the growing margin of the plate, the far edge is sliding downward. Older plate rock is being devoured while new plate rock is being formed. It is like a conveyor belt. That is why none of the rock forming the floor of the ocean basins today is older than the Jurassic Period, about 180 million years old. Almost all ocean floor crust is much younger, some being formed even as you read this. What a startling fact, considering that the Earth is over 4.5 billion years old: that the ocean basins as we now know them should be so young.

It just stands to reason that if the ocean basins are not all that old, and if they are continually changing in shape, the geography of continents must be changing also. That is what happens through continental drift. Rocks making up the continents are less dense than the rocks that form the bulk of the plates, causing the continental crust to float—like ice cubes in a tall glass of cool Texas iced tea—on the heavier plate rock. As the plates grow and subduct, the continents float on top. It is as if the continents were resting on conveyor belts.

That is the concept of continental drift. It explains why the east coast of South America seems as if it would fit into the west coast of Africa like a puzzle. The reason is, of course, because they used to do just that but have now drifted apart. Their outlines are a clue to their geographic history. Where plates converge and continents collide, huge mountains are formed, like the Himalayas, for example.

The implications of continental drift and its plate tectonic mechanism are profound. It means the Earth is ever-changing in a very proactive way. The size of oceans and their distribution over the globe are products of Earth processes. The geographic arrangement of continents is, too. Even something that appears so unrelated as the weather is part and parcel of this because weather is controlled by the distribution of solar heat across the globe. The distribution of solar heat is accomplished by oceanic and atmospheric currents, the details of which are determined by the position of the continents and oceans. If those change, climate will be modified, and so will life along with it.

The climates of continents are also controlled by the latitudes where they are found: lands near polar latitudes are naturally colder than those closer to the equator. As continents drift through latitudes over geologic time, their climatic regimes are altered. Finally, the lay of the land—the presence of mountains and valleys like those formed through plate tectonics—will influence the climate on a regional or local scale. All of this ensures that environments change through geologic time. That affects life on Earth.

Speaking casually, the rate of continental drift does not appear to be all that fast: about the speed that your fingernails grow. But multiply that times the number of years that the dinosaurs reigned and you will see that the continents could be moved hundreds or thousands of miles from a spreading center. They could collide and coalesce; they could split apart. As a matter of fact, that is exactly what they did in their drifting odyssey.

What does all this mean for Texas dinosaurs? It means that we cannot look back into the past and hope to recognize the political boundaries that now define Texas. We cannot even hope to recognize the physical boundaries like the Rio Grande or the Red River or the Llano Estacado. They simply were not there during the time of the dinosaurs. Moreover, we should not expect the continental outline of North America to be as it is now when we journey so far back into the past. It was not the same. It was not even the same between each of the three time intervals that now provide us with Texas dinosaur fossils. Those dinosaurs whose remains are now found in the rocks of the Panhandle lived in a very different world and at a very different time from those found in Central Texas, and the same is true when those two are compared to Big Bend fossils. Not only did they live at different times and in different continental geographies, but the dinosaurs are also completely different species in each of the three areas.

So there you have it. That is why Texas dinosaurs are significant. They represent a varied sampling of dinosaur diversity. They lived at three distinct intervals during the Age of Dinosaurs. And they lived in such different arrangements of the continents and oceans that they may as well have lived in different worlds. In a sense, they did inhabit three separate worlds—at least, we can think of them that way. We can think of the three worlds of Texas dinosaurs, investigate each in turn, see how their stories fit together, and revel in what they tell us about the history of life on our planet. That is how we will proceed.

It is a Texas legacy from worlds long past.

CHAPTER 2

The Original Homestead

THE FIRST WORLD OF TEXAS DINOSAURS began well over 200 million years ago in the Late Triassic, the oldest of the three periods of the Age of Reptiles. It was near in time to the evolutionary origin of dinosaurs. Very early in their history dinosaurs were small and rare, but they roamed over most of the Earth's land surface. At the time, all of the continents were united into one land mass. This was the original homestead: a giant supercontinent called Pangea.

Because all the major land areas of the Earth were conjoined, it is simple to imagine that ground-dwelling animals might easily walk from place to place, each species expanding its range as ecological and environmental conditions permitted. If that is so, then the fossils of Pangea should be more or less similar wherever they are found in rocks of the same age on the remnants of the supercontinent. To a large extent, that is what we see from studying the fossil record. However, Pangea was a big place, stretching both north and south from the equator and crossing many zones of climate. Moreover, such a great land mass creates its own diversity of ecological conditions from one region to another. Thus, the environment was not the same over the geographic extent of the land; and, of course, different environments support varying suites of life. Nevertheless, dinosaur fossils are known over much of Pangea very early in the history of the group. The most precisely dated early dinosaurs are found in what is now Argentina and are approximately 230 million years old. Dinosaurs are not known from Texas until around 220 million years ago, perhaps a bit more: several million years after their first dated occurrence in South America.

Early in their history, dinosaurs were small and not at all the dominant life forms we think of when we hear the word. But it makes sense. The fossil record often shows that the earliest members of a group are smaller than later species that seem to be more common and more diverse. The evolution of larger-sized descendants from smaller-sized ancestors is so common a phenomenon that it is called Cope's Rule (named for Edward Drinker Cope). Along with the evolution of a greater range in size comes an increase in the number of species. This is a generality, but it makes sense in that the evolution of new species must start with a single ancestral species.

The oldest well-dated dinosaurs are *Eoraptor lunensis* (EE-oh-RAP-tur loo-NEN-sis) and *Herrerasaurus ischigualastensis* (huh-RAYR-uh-SAWR-us ISH-ee-gwuh-las-TEN-sis). Those are great-sounding words once you get your tongue trained. *Eoraptor* means "dawn plunderer" because it was a carnivore and lived at the beginning of dinosaur history. *Lunensis* is a reference to where it was found: Valley of the Moon, Ischigualasto Provincial Park, Argentina. *Herrerasaurus ischigualastensis* was named for Victorino Herrera, a paleontologist, and for Ischigualasto Park. Its remains were discovered prior to those of *Eoraptor* but in the same area. The two species were contemporaries. Both are carnivorous theropod saurischians, but *Eoraptor* is more primitive because its skull lacks specializations seen in other theropods. It is the rest of the skeleton, not the skull, that provides the clues to its theropod relationships.

In the same park as the carnivores but in slightly younger rocks, another dinosaur, *Pisanosaurus mertii* (pye-SAN-uh-SAWR-us MUR-tee-eye), was found. *Pisanosaurus* is the earliest-known ornithischian. From *Pisanosaurus, Eoraptor,* and *Herrerasaurus* at Ischigualasto we know that the initial evolutionary branching that led to the major groups of dinosaurs that later dominated the world occurred very early in dinosaur history. There were even some South American animals that might be dinosaurs but are too primitive to fit into either the ornithischian or saurischian groups—all the more evidence that a time near the origin of dinosaurs is being sampled at Ischigualasto.

Alongside the early dinosaurs at Ischigualasto lived an amazing variety of nondinosaurian carnivorous and herbivorous reptiles, strange amphibians, and even mammal relatives. The dinosaurs as a group were certainly not the masters of the Ischigualasto ecosystem. They were simply a part of it.

Even though we know a great deal about early dinosaurs from their fossil record in Argentina, it is not certain that South America is the exact cradle of their origin because they are found quite early in other parts of Pangea. These other occurrences are certainly relevant to the issue. So where is the cradle of dinosaur origins? We need more fossils and better dating to expect a satisfying answer. Why did dinosaurs evolve when they did? That is also a good question and another line of research for future paleontologists because we simply do not yet know. It is unclear what specific environmental factors, if any, brought about the evolutionary origin of dinosaurs. Nor does anyone know for sure exactly why early dinosaurs split into the evolutionary lineages that led to all the herbivorous bird-hipped ornithischians, the carnivorous theropods, and the gigantic sauropodomorphs. Nevertheless, one thing is sure: they did. And what is more, they did it very soon after the evolutionary origin of dinosaurs from nondinosaurian ancestors. The fossils of South America tell us that. Therefore, if our Texas rocks are younger than those in South America, the dinosaurs found in them could belong to any of the major groups. As dinosaurs dispersed across Pangea from wherever they started to where they ended up, they were evolving into new species of the greatest group of reptiles the world has ever seen.

The Earth's land masses may have been joined together into Pangea during the Triassic Period, allowing the inhabitants potential access to real estate, but that does not mean the Earth's internal forces had ceased their inexorable drive to rearrange the world's geography. The processes of plate tectonics were at work to disintegrate Pangea, just as they had worked to form it. In the western part of what would become North America, rivers and lakes deposited sediments. What was to become the American East Coast, while it lay in the middle of the supercontinent, was obtrusively beginning to form. It was a rift valley, the superficial expression of the supercontinent being ripped apart. What was to be the eastern United States was beginning to diverge from northwestern Africa. The Atlantic Ocean was soon to begin its filling. We know all this from the rocks.

When geologists want to make sense out of rocks and the fossils contained in them, one of the first things they do is make a map. Geologic maps are pictures of rocks, most commonly drawn as if the artist—in this case, geologist—were looking down on them with a bird's eye view. Maps show the geometric relationships of one rock unit to another. They provide evidence of geologic time by presenting clear representations of superposition of rock layers, of past geography and environments through the kinds of rocks being mapped, and of events throughout the Earth's history as shown by faults, volcanoes, and other structures that cut through the rock layers. That is how the geologic history of North America was chronicled. Making maps is one of the things at which Robert T. Hill, the father of Texas geology, excelled.

The arrangements of rocks as drawn on a map are what remains as evidence of all the sedimentological, erosional, and structural changes that previously happened in the region. Each rock formation that is large enough to be mapped is named, usually after some geographic feature or a characteristic kind of rock that makes it up. Formations can be lumped together with other closely related rock formations into formal groups. Each formation on a geologic map is usually indicated by a different color. The color patterns show how the rock units fit with each other; from that, a good part of their geological history can be interpreted.

The oldest dinosaurs in Texas—220 million years old—are from red rock strata called the Dockum Group, named after a small nineteenth-century Panhandle town east of Lubbock in Dickens County. Cummins and Cope visited there. The Dockum Group is a series of sand, silt, and mud formations deposited by lakes and rivers in a big, low depositional basin that was much later to become West Texas and eastern New Mexico. Sediments from surrounding uplands were carried to the basin by rivers and streams. The basin probably had no outlet to the sea, like the Great Basin of Utah and Nevada today. As the sediments built up, they buried and entombed the carcasses and bones that have become the fossils we study and admire.

The Dockum basin was a much different geological setting from that of the contemporaneous rift valley that was to become the American East. It was more similar to conditions that existed in the other direction, in what was to become the western states. It was particularly like Arizona, with its similarly aged rocks that now glorify the Painted Desert and Petrified Forest. All the way from Texas, through New Mexico to Arizona, the crimson rocks of the Triassic burn on the horizon. And there are fossils the whole way.

Twenty years ago, when Phil Murry, then a graduate student at SMU, first went to prospect for fossils in the bright red silts, muds, and sands of the Dockum, he expected to see it overlain by a characteristic white limestone. He knew that in some places white marine limestones of Cretaceous age rested on the Triassic red beds of the Dockum. He had seen it represented on geologic maps. Phil was doing his prospecting at a place called Otis Chalk near Big Spring in Howard County. Since chalk is a kind of limestone made from the bodies of tiny ocean-dwelling organisms and Otis sounded as though it could be the name of a place, Phil understandably figured Otis Chalk was the name of a rock formation. He was puzzled that he had not seen the name on a map. As it turns out, much to Phil's amusement, Otis Chalk is not a rock formation but the name of the rancher who owned the land so rich in Dockum Group bones. The fossil sites around the land he worked are called the Otis Chalk localities.

Otis Chalk is not the only place where the Dockum Group outcrops in Texas. There is a Texas-sized ring of exposures from north of Amarillo along the breaks of the Canadian River, and to the south and east where Dockum strata lie bare along the walls of Palo Duro Canyon. It continues south to the area east of Lubbock where the standard of Dockum rocks is located and then on to the base of the Panhandle near Big Spring. The ring of Triassic rock continues on around through eastern New Mexico. Enclosed in this ring is the Llano Estacado (the Staked Plains), the broad, flat limit of the southern High Plains described in the first chapter.

The passage of time represented by Dockum rocks is on the order of millions of years. That is plenty of time for the evolution of new species, for the extinction of old ones, for climates to change in minor or major ways, and for different species to move in and set up residence in the Dockum basin. We should not expect all the fossils from the Dockum to be of exactly the same age if they happen not to be collected from the same spot.

The Dockum is rich in fossils of many kinds. There are plants, together with an abundance of species of animals. Most importantly for us, there are dinosaurs. But there are not many. Throughout the time interval represented by the Dockum, dinosaurs appear to have been minor players on the Triassic ecological stage. That was true here, just as it was at Ischigualasto. We know little of what most Dockum dinosaurs were like, but we can supplement our knowledge with what we know of other dinosaurs of similar age from New Mexico and Arizona.

The most primitive dinosaur known from the Texas Dockum is a brand-new one called *Chindesaurus* (chin-de-SAWR-us). A part of the pelvis was discovered in Crosby County east of Lubbock by a Michigan field party led by E. C. Case. There is also a thigh bone known from Howard County near Big Spring, but most of the fossils of *Chindesaurus* are from Arizona. Although it is not well known, *Chindesaurus* is interesting because it is most similar to the South American *Eoraptor* and *Herrerasaurus,* the earliest dated theropods from the beginning of dinosaur history.

Other dinosaurs from the Texas Dockum are similarly poorly known, but we know enough about them to know that there are several different species present. Perhaps the best known of all Triassic dinosaurs in North America is the small, carnivorous saurischian *Coelophysis bauri* (SEE-luh-FYE-sis BOW-er-eye). (This dinosaur was recently renamed *Rioarribasaurus colberti* [REE-oh-uh-REE-buh-SAWR-us KOL-burt-eye] to conform to trivial nomenclatural legalities. Which name to use is a bit up in the air right now. The community of dinosaur paleontologists is awaiting an official decision as to which name is valid. It makes sense to me to use *Coelophysis,* so I will.) *Coelophysis* may be the best known of North American Triassic dinosaurs, but it is not common in Texas. Although there are scattered discoveries of scraps of bone and teeth isolated from their jaws that have been referred to *Coelophysis,* it is hard to say for sure which species of animal they belonged to because the parts we have simply are not very diagnostic. Nevertheless, it is very likely that *Coelophysis* would have inhabited the Texas landscape in Triassic times.

The really good specimens of *Coelophysis* come from Ghost Ranch, New Mexico, from a quarry found in 1947 by American Museum field parties under the direction of the great Edwin Harris Colbert, one of the finest pale-ontologists of this century. Cope (there is that name again) originally de-scribed this dinosaur in the last century based on fragments of bone sent to him from New Mexico. Colbert went back to the area where he reckoned the first specimens were found, and the result was a quarry that yielded com-plete skeletons in abundance. Remains of at least a thousand individuals of the species were coaxed from the red riverine mud of the baked hillside and out into the bright twentieth-century New Mexico sun. The specimens range from hatchlings to full-grown adults, a cross section of the population. Skel-etons lay in grotesque death poses, their bodies intertwined. Almost all the bones found in the quarry are of *Coelophysis;* very few remains of other spe-cies have been found there.

How could such a concentration of dinosaur fossils have been formed? "Elementary, my dear Watson."

With paleontology, as with all science, we must take the attitude of Sherlock Holmes, realizing that the story of Ghost Ranch is woven into the rocks and fossils we have at our disposal. Clues come from the fossils them-selves and from the sediments that entomb them.

Just as important as knowing about sediments is a knowledge of how animals die and how their bodies become concentrated together nowadays. Although it may seem macabre, it is essential to understanding how fossil deposits are formed. There is, in fact, an entire book, first published in 1927, dedicated to an evaluation of modern carcasses in southern Texas. It was writ-ten by Johannes Weigelt, who came from Europe to observe depositional environments in Louisiana, Oklahoma, and Texas. Most of his time was spent along the Gulf Coast from New Orleans to Matagorda Bay, halfway down the Texas coast. The meat of the book (please excuse the pun) is based on his observations of a mass death of fish, turtles, and alligators at Smithers Lake in Fort Bend County. Smithers Lake is still there, west of Houston, nestled in a bend of the Brazos, east and just a little south of the county seat at Richmond. The mass death at Smithers Lake was caused by a sudden drop in temperature when a norther blew across the Gulf Coast in December, 1924. If you were around that area on Christmas, 1989, when Galveston Bay froze, you can imagine what it must have been like during the freeze at Smithers Lake. Weigelt documented not only how animals die but what happens to their carcasses afterward, and he provided specific examples of similar phenomena from the fossil record.

To understand the *Coelophysis* Quarry at Ghost Ranch, let us begin by examining the bones for evidence. The first clue is simply that there are so many of one kind of animal found in the quarry. Why should that be? Whatever conditions formed the fossil deposit were clearly concentrating the bones of a single group, one population. Members of the population interacted with each other. We know that from the not-so-pleasant recognition of the bones of young *Coelophysis* in the stomach region of larger ones: *Coelophysis* was a cannibal.

Taken as a whole, the sizes of the individuals represented by the bones indicate yearly age classes. What that means is that *Coelophysis* probably had a discrete breeding season so that the young of one season are of similar size but smaller than the young of the previous season, which in turn are smaller than those hatched the season before, and so on until adult size is reached. Moreover, since there are all ages represented, whatever killed the animals was indiscriminate with respect to age, selecting neither the young nor the old exclusively. Some individuals are slender and others more robust, possibly representing the difference between males and females. All ages and both sexes were affected equally by the killing agent.

The next clue as to how this fossil concentration was formed is derived from the fact that many of the skeletons are complete or nearly so. That means that a goodly number of the corpses were buried whole, and those that were not had not been greatly scattered.

The positions of the skeletons are telling as well. In some, their long necks and tails are recurved over the body, indicating that the remains lay exposed to the air before burial. This allowed the sinews to dry and shrink, arching the head and tail over the torso. The jaws are tightly closed. There is little evidence of scavenging despite their exposure. From that we can conclude that the animals all died at about the same time and their carcasses did not stay on the surface long before they were entombed. Because the legs, tails, and necks of so many skeletons are intertwined and because all the bones are fossilized in the same way, they not only died at the same time, they were buried all at once. The skeletons are often more or less aligned with each other in similar directions. That sort of arrangement provides more clues to the processes involved from death to burial.

But how did they get buried? We must consider the sediments. All of the rock in the *Coelophysis* Quarry was deposited as mud, silt, or sand by an ancient river. There are nodules of lime of the kind found in soils formed in seasonal environments. The nodules were not formed at the site. They were eroded from their place of origin and moved along with the river sediments to be deposited along with the silt and mud. The quarry is predominantly red, except for some splotches where the rusty iron color was reduced to green by the roots and remains of ancient plants, now long gone, and by percolating water in the sediments after the bone deposit had been formed.

Thus, we know from the rocks that the climate was seasonal because seasonality is reflected by the soil nodules. That conclusion is supported by the incremental growth seen in *Coelophysis* that is interpreted to indicate seasonal breeding. Seasonal climates suffer droughts, which can seriously stress populations of animals, forcing them to congregate around dwindling water supplies, weakening them to the point that they are more susceptible than usual to disease and to the other hazards of life.

Think about it as if that were the case with *Coelophysis*. Drought brought the animals together near shrinking supplies of water, then torturingly sapped the life from the screeching, bickering flock. Even if water were plentiful, if it had been the best of times, it would have been hard for such a large troop of meat eaters to find sufficient food in one place. As carnivores, they would have been aggressive from the start. Given the situation, their aggression turned fiercely on each other. Under stress, the larger ones turned to eating the small. But it did not help them much. This population of *Coelophysis* could not survive what nature had in store for it. So many stressed theropods—over a thousand—all in one parched area, trampling to mud the remnants of what was once their source of life-giving water, scratching the mud to scorching dust as it dried—and then they succumbed. They began to die. How could these beasts have avoided the suffering imposed on them by the harsh circumstances of nature?

Only then did the rains come, but it was too late for a host of the *Coelophysis* population. The skies clouded and the drought broke. Dark rain clouds regurgitated the water that they would not yield when it was needed most. The rain poured in torrents, eroding the earth, caking the dust formed in the drought, lifting it and whipping it into frothy currents. The rivers swelled to capacity. Their sediment load was immense. *Coelophysis* bodies were picked up and whisked into the flow. They bobbed and bounced. As the current waned, carcasses clogged the stream channel as African wildebeest do today in the floods of the Mara River in Kenya. The *Coelophysis* bodies came to rest, partially aligned with the current. The clouds withdrew. The waters subsided. Whatever survivors there may have been straggled off to struggle for survival another day.

In the heat of the sun, the *Coelophysis* corpses began to dry out. Their fluids evaporated, their sinews shrank, their necks drew back. Soon they were covered with silt, leaving them protected until erosion would bring them to the surface—and to the eyes of paleontologists—some 220 million years later.

Is that really what happened at Ghost Ranch? Perhaps it is. Some set of circumstances led to the formation of the *Coelophysis* Quarry, and a drought followed by a flood seems most likely, especially in a seasonal climate. Most importantly, the drought hypothesis is consistent with all the evidence at hand, both geological and paleontological. It is also consistent with observations we can make on wildlife today, although at first it may not appear so. For instance, modern carnivores do not congregate in vast herds; herbivores do. Great herds of bison used to stretch across the plains for miles. In Africa today, huge numbers of wildebeest migrate together across the Serengeti Plain. Periodically they stampede into swollen rivers, resulting in tremendous mortality and potential future fossil deposits. It is difficult to imagine such a situation occurring with modern carnivores. But then again, these dinosaurs were not modern carnivores. There is possibly, however, a much more appropriate example from the modern world with which we might compare the accumulation of *Coelophysis*. Severe drought near the mouth of the Amazon once caused the death of eight thousand crocodilians in one area.

One of the most significant things about *Coelophysis* is that it is so well known from the Ghost Ranch skeletons that knowledge of it provides a reasonable model for early theropods in general. In particular, the recovery of bones, cracked and warped from the compression of the sediments for 220 million years after their burial, allows us to imagine what *Coelophysis* may have been like in life.

Coelophysis was a rather small theropod. The adults were about nine or ten feet long, with sharp, serrated, bladelike teeth set in strong, slender jaws. The elongate head was rather small but narrow and pointed, and set atop a sinuous neck. The forelimbs, roughly half the length of the hind limbs, ended in three talonlike fingers armed with sharp, curved claws, always at the ready for grasping, scratching, or tearing. The hips balanced on the hind legs. The legs were long for transporting the slim body with sprightly steps. *Coelophysis* bounced along on three toes, each with a curved claw. A fourth toe, the dew claw, did not reach the ground. The back was held nearly horizontally, the neck curved up in a gracile "S" to the head. The long tail was held out behind as a counterbalance.

As a small, active carnivore, *Coelophysis* probably ate whatever it could run down with its speeding hind legs. Its diet probably included small, lizardlike animals, plus anything else that it could subdue with the snapping jaws extended from its darting neck. And, of course, there is the evidence that *Coelophysis* was a cannibal, at least when times got tough. Specimens at

*Carcasses of the rhino-
ceroslike herbivore*
Placerias *clog the channel
of a stream as flood waters
recede. The soft tissue rots
away and the skeletons
become entombed in
sediments. This is one way
in which fossil deposits are
formed. Illustration by
Karen Carr.*

Ghost Ranch show that smaller *Coelophysis* might have made a meal for larger ones because small *Coelophysis* bones are preserved in the stomach region of some of the larger skeletons. Other reptiles, such as crocodiles and Komodo dragons (a kind of large lizard), will opportunistically gobble up their young. Some mammals and birds are known to do so as well. It would not be surprising if *Coelophysis* did.

The young of the species may have relied more on insects than on smaller vertebrates for sustenance, just as the diet of crocodiles changes as they grow larger. Small crocodiles consume a large percentage of insects, but as they get bigger, so does their preferred prey. As *Coelophysis* got older and larger, the size of its prey may have increased also. It is unclear what sort of social behavior *Coelophysis* had. Carnivores are generally less sociable than herbivores—it does not pay to hang around with something that might eat you—but many species of mammalian carnivores form packs or prides or family groups. Crocodiles congregate along stretches of riverbanks. For courtship and mating, and probably in nesting and hatching, *Coelophysis* could be found in groups of greater or smaller size, but the exact size of the social groups is hard to say. Unless they were like some birds that occasionally form enormous flocks, it is most likely that the huge assemblage represented at Ghost Ranch was together more because of the extremes of the environment caused by drought than because of normal social interaction in the species.

Herbivorous bird-hipped dinosaurs are less well known than carnivorous lizard-hipped dinosaurs in the North American Triassic. Although ornithischians were around, they are not common as fossils, nor are there samples from anywhere that approach the quality of Ghost Ranch. The earliest known dinosaur herbivores have simple, leaf-shaped teeth with denticles along the edges. Such a tooth design is found both in early sauropodomorphs, which are saurischians, and in early ornithischians, so it can be hard to tell the difference if the samples at hand include only isolated teeth or scraps of jaws. Even some geologically younger herbivores, like stegosaurs and ankylosaurs (both ornithischians), have teeth with a similar leaf shape.

Leaf-shaped teeth found in New Mexico have been named *Revueltosaurus callenderi* (REV-yoo-EL-tuh-SAWR-us KAL-en-duhr-eye). Across the border to the east, similar teeth have been found in the Texas Dockum. Although these teeth are probably those of an ornithischian dinosaur, there is very little more that can be said about them until the mouths that they fell out of become known and can be thoroughly studied. You see, exciting discoveries are waiting to be made.

Efficient chewing or chopping of tough vegetation requires that the teeth come into contact with each other when the jaws close so that they can shear

Coelophysis may have been a dinosaur cannibal, at least during hard times. Bones of small ones are found in the stomach regions of large ones. Here, two hungry adults fight over the remains of a baby. Illustration by Karen Carr.

the food in the mouth. Leaf-shaped teeth had relatively little tooth-to-tooth contact when chewing, and what they had was of a functionally simple nature. This indicates that the earliest dinosaurian herbivores were limited to a diet of rather soft vegetation. They did not have a sophisticated method of chewing their food, nor did they have the dental batteries composed of numerous rapidly replaced teeth seen in many later dinosaurian herbivores. They probably did have cheeks, which was a major evolutionary advance. Extensive food processing by chewing requires cheeks to keep the food from falling out of the sides of the mouth. Ornithischians developed cheeks early in their history. From what we can tell of early ornithischians, they were bipedal in addition to being herbivorous. Their bodies were not greatly different in shape from *Coelophysis,* although their heads were shorter.

The only plant eater named from the Texas Dockum is called *Techno-*

saurus smalli (TECK-nuh-SAWR-us SMAWL-eye), named by Sankar Chatterjee for Texas Tech University, where he teaches. *Technosaurus* is known from a lower jaw, part of an upper jaw, and a couple of bones farther back in the skeleton. All of the pieces were found together. The teeth in the jaw fragments are small and leaf-shaped, so it is fairly certain that *Technosaurus* was a herbivore. Chatterjee recognized it as an ornithischian. Later, the identification of part of the specimen, an upper jaw fragment, was questioned and suggested to be from a prosauropod. If that is true, then the bones of *Technosaurus* are represented by a mixed bag of fossils: some from a primitive ornithischian and others from a primitive prosauropod saurischian. The identity of *Technosaurus* as an ornithischian or as the mingled remains of both an ornithischian and a prosauropod are alternative published interpretations of the scant evidence now available. Prosauropod fossils have been found in nearby New Mexico and Arizona, although they are rare in both places. Leaving alternative interpretations of *Technosaurus* aside, the Dockum landscape was clearly inhabited by early ornithischian herbivores, and it would not be surprising if prosauropods lived there, too.

Technosaurus was discovered at a locality known as the Post Quarry in Garza County, near the town of Post and southeast of Lubbock. The quarry was first worked by the Dallas Museum of Natural History in a preliminary way, then by Chatterjee and his crews from Texas Tech, who have labored extensively. They have amassed a wonderful collection and a great wealth of interesting fossils. While the Texas Dockum has yielded many fossils from many places to the scrutinizing eyes of paleontologists, the Post Quarry now holds the position as the most impressive fossil locality in the Texas Triassic, just as Ghost Ranch has that honor in New Mexico. Although the geological evidence for the formation of the Post Quarry has not been so extensively studied as that of Ghost Ranch, and even though both quarries occur in red riverine muds now hardened to soft stone, there are clearly some differences between the two.

Most striking are the differences in the species represented. Post may be similar in age to the Ghost Ranch Quarry, but the animals are very different between the two, and no *Coelophysis* is yet known from Post. At Ghost Ranch, most fossils are of *Coelophysis,* with few other species represented. At the Post Quarry, the fauna is diverse with at least fourteen species represented, but it is not overly dominated by any particular one. Three or four species are dinosaurs, two of which have been named. A few of the other species have been studied, but not all of them, and probably none has yet been studied in the depth and detail that all of them will be in time. Most species at Post are either archaic, large-headed amphibians or belong to reptile groups other than the Dinosauria. They will be discussed in detail shortly. It is significant in the comparison with Ghost Ranch, however, to note that quite a mixture of species is represented, and those species present in the quarry probably inhabited a variety of environments. The amphibians and some of the reptiles are likely to have lived in low, moist areas like ponds and riverbanks, while the dinosaurs and most of the other reptiles appear better suited for life in drier, well-drained, more upland areas, frequenting water sources only as necessary.

Another difference between Post and Ghost Ranch is that few, if any, of the Post specimens are complete skeletons. While bones of a single individual occasionally appear to be associated, they are rarely articulated and attached as they were in life. There are massive bones and there are delicate bones. A greater total size range is represented by all the individuals at Post as compared to the *Coelophysis* Quarry. No single species at Post is represented in numbers anywhere near approaching those of *Coelophysis* at Ghost Ranch, although the total number of specimens at the Post Quarry will probably turn out to be equally as impressive as that at the *Coelophysis* Quarry.

Although there are differences between the two fossil localities, there are some important similarities, too. Bones at the Post Quarry occur in red mudstone, as at Ghost Ranch. There is little evidence of scavenging (except, perhaps, for the disarticulation of skeletons at Post). Some of the bones appear to have been aligned in similar directions during deposition. There is a diversity in size, both in having the young and old of a single species and in having very small and large species together. Carnivores appear to outnumber herbivores at Post, even with all its diversity.

Chatterjee interprets the Post Quarry assemblage as the consequence of a single event, perhaps a flash flood, which caused the death of many individuals of many species. Rapid, rushing water drowned the victims, mixing their bodies and gathering them in one place along a river channel. As the carcasses rotted over a period of days or weeks, currents winnowed away the bones and body parts that could be transported downstream and aligned many of the remaining bones with the direction of the current. Then, as the currents dwindled, mud fell out of suspension, covering and protecting the bones and preserving them until they were extricated by paleontologists. The main difference in this scenario from that of Ghost Ranch is that flooding, not drought, is invoked as the catastrophic agent in the formation of the quarry.

The Post Quarry is not only unlike the *Coelophysis* Quarry in the kinds of animals found there, it is also strangely different from fossil localities in the rest of the Texas Dockum. One reason is that it is probably slightly younger than most of the other Texas Triassic localities, which would explain part of the uniqueness of its animal life. Other aspects of its singularity are not so easy to explain. Take, for instance, the amazing little creature, supposedly a dinosaur, named *Shuvosaurus inexpectatus* (SHOOV-uh-SAWR-us in-ecks-peck-TATE-us) by Chatterjee. The name is for his son who cleaned and prepared it in the laboratory, and because *Shuvosaurus* has features of the skeleton that were completely unexpected. *Shuvosaurus,* as described by Chatterjee, is a theropod saurischian. Such beasts are usually discussed as lizard-hipped, bipedal, carnivorous dinosaurs. But *Shuvosaurus* has no teeth. That is not necessarily strange, because a few other groups of theropods—the ostrich mimics, or ornithomimisaurs, for example—are lizard-hipped, bipedal, carnivorous dinosaurs with species having no teeth. However, *Shuvosaurus* has other, even stranger, features that go along with its edentulous jaws. It was not even carnivorous.

Not much is known of the skeleton of *Shuvosaurus,* but there is a skull and a presumed portion of the hind leg. Its hind legs, if correctly associated with the skull, were long and thin. For a dinosaur, *Shuvosaurus* is a small one. The skull is about six inches long, but the eye sockets are enormous. The jaws were powerful, and it had a short, heavy beak. The front edges of the beak were sharp. A platform was formed in the floor of the mouth at the front end of the lower jaw. It appears from the jaws of *Shuvosaurus* that it had some of the same adaptations as seed-eating birds. Perhaps it gained its nourishment in a similar way, using the sharp edges of its beak to slice soft vegetation and its nutcracker for more durable plant food, perhaps seeds.

Much of Chatterjee's description of *Shuvosaurus* would apply equally to ostrich dinosaurs, so it is possible that *Shuvosaurus* is itself one. That is what is so strange about it. At the beginning of this chapter, there is a long discussion about the Triassic origin of dinosaurs and how the earliest species are so primitive. Well, *Shuvosaurus* is not primitive at all. The ostrich dinosaurs, which it seems to resemble most, lived toward the end of the of the Age of Dinosaurs, with records in the Late Jurassic but mostly in the Cretaceous. That is on the order of seventy-five million years after *Shuvosaurus!*

How can that be explained? Either *Shuvosaurus* is a theropod saurischian of the ostrich-mimic dinosaur group, or it is not. If it is not, what is it? If it is, how did the most advanced of the ostrich dinosaurs end up where the most primitive of dinosaurs should be? Chatterjee offered two alternative explanations. Perhaps *Shuvosaurus* is not an ostrich-mimic dinosaur but rather a different kind of ruling reptile that evolved characters confusingly similar to the ostrich mimics. It would be a strange case of convergent evolution: *Shuvosaurus* and ostrich mimics evolving from distinct ancestors that did not closely resemble each other, producing descendants with similar features shaped by natural selection and the ecological constraints of their way of life. Under this interpretation, *Shuvosaurus* and ostrich mimics ended up looking like each other even though they are not closely related. Convergent evolution is not uncommon in the history of life, and we will return to another example of it shortly.

The other explanation of the relationships of *Shuvosaurus* as presented by Chatterjee is that it really is an ostrich-mimic dinosaur, and its early occurrence is a humbling lesson on the inadequacy of the fossil record. That is also a possibility. No one would argue that the fossil record as we know it is fully complete. It is spotty with respect to the species represented, environments preserved, geographic area, and geologic time. There are clearly great opportunities for field research. On the other hand, depending on the question being asked of it, the fossil record can place real and meaningful constraints on how we view the history of life. The data of the fossil record, like evidence in a court of law, must be used prudently.

Has *Shuvosaurus* been studied thoroughly enough—and have ostrich-mimic dinosaurs in general been studied thoroughly enough—to fully evaluate this curious situation? Probably not. It will not do, however, to dismiss *Shuvosaurus* as simply a case of misidentification or human error because *Shuvosaurus* is certainly something, and something very strange at that. Just what it is—that is what we want to know. If more specimens are needed to solve the riddle, more fieldwork will bring the answer to light, and I suspect that is how the solution will come. More fieldwork should produce more and perhaps better specimens, including at least parts of the skeleton that are not now known, all placed in clear geological context. That would give us more pieces to this fascinating paleontological puzzle.

For now I am dubious about *Shuvosaurus.* Much of the paleontological community appears to be. The reason is because *Shuvosaurus,* as an ostrich mimic, is just so out of place—out of time—that judgment on it as an ornithomimisaur, or even a dinosaur, must be reserved until more of the skeleton is known and its relationships are more adequately supported. Nevertheless, *Shuvosaurus,* whatever it is, is very interesting. There are a lot of interesting beasts in the Dockum. During the Triassic Period, there were some nondinosaurian groups of reptiles that were very specialized in a number of ways. Perhaps *Shuvosaurus* is related to one of them.

On top of all that, *Shuvosaurus* is not the only dinosaurian puzzle from Post. There is this matter of the proposed earliest bird, *Protoavis* (pro-toe-AVE-us). There is strong logic to the notion that birds are descended from theropods. Accepting that as being so, birds can be accommodated in the big group of animals called saurischian dinosaurs. They are specialized members of the group, just as *Diplodocus* and other sauropods make up a different branch of specialized saurischians. The bird branch is separate and distinct from them but originated in all probability from within the theropods. We will return to that topic in the final chapter, where it will be justified further. For now we will accept birds as dinosaurs and discuss the implications of finding *Protoavis* at the Post Quarry. *Protoavis* caused quite a stir in the paleontological community.

According to Chatterjee, *Protoavis* was a pheasant-sized bird. It is not exactly like modern birds because it has teeth at the front end of the mouth and a bony tail. It also has four fingers. As reconstructed, the skull is quite birdlike with a big brain. An enlarged brain presumably facilitated its sense of balance, coordination, agility, and high level of activity, all of which are necessary in a flying vertebrate. It may have been able to hear quite well. The orbits, or eye sockets, are large and directed forward, as in modern birds of prey. Eyes turned forward in the skull facilitate binocular vision. Chatterjee interpreted *Protoavis* as a visually oriented predator with vocally oriented behavior. Other features he points to that define *Protoavis* as a bird are an upper jaw that moves, neck vertebrae that permitted a wide range of motion, and various adaptations for flight.

If *Protoavis* is truly a bird—and for many paleontologists that is quite a big if—then it, too, seems out of its time. After all, *Archaeopteryx* (ar-kee-OP-ter-icks) did not live until 150 million years ago, perhaps 75 million years after *Protoavis*; yet *Protoavis* is described as being more like modern birds than *Archaeopteryx*. It is a situation analogous to *Shuvosaurus* being of an anomalous age. It is a red flag. It is not impossible that the vicissitudes of the fossil record should produce such a picture of bird evolution, it is just strange.

In science, huge anomalies, such as the cases of *Protoavis* and *Shuvosaurus*, are trying to tell us something. Either the hypotheses of bird and dinosaur evolution are all wet, or there is something wrong with the identifications. It would not do to take a reckless and cavalier approach, throwing away all that we have learned without overwhelming proof to the contrary. On the other hand, we should not stay wedded to outmoded ideas.

The main criticisms leveled at *Protoavis* deal with whether or not all of the bones assigned to it really belong to one and the same species, whether the bones of several species have been mixed, or whether the quality of the specimens is adequate to support Chatterjee's claims. No studies have yet been published justifying any of the criticisms. Most of the censure has come through the popular press. And if we were to be quite frank, some of the criticisms of Chatterjee and *Protoavis* have an effete aroma of arrogance. Although reasonable skepticism is healthy in science, unreasonable cynicism is unbecoming for the profession. Still, the burden of proof has to remain on

Chatterjee to produce a compelling case for his contentions, even to the most cynical of his detractors, or he must abandon his hypotheses and find a better explanation of his data. That is the way science works. Nevertheless, whether belonging to one animal called *Protoavis* or to more than one, the bones from Post still belong to something. If not *Protoavis,* then what?

To tell you the truth, I find the concept of a Triassic bird less troublesome than that of a Triassic ornithomimosaurid. After all, the early fossil record of birds is admittedly abysmal by almost any standard, the excellent skeletons with preserved feather impressions of *Archaeopteryx* notwithstanding. It would not be too surprising to learn that birds originated about the same time as some other dinosaur groups. But a Triassic ornithomimosaurid! And one even more derived and specialized than those that lived at the end of the Age of Dinosaurs. How can that be? We know much more about Triassic, Jurassic, and Cretaceous dinosaurs than we do about fossil birds. Can we have gone so wrong? The answer to that is, quite surely, yes, we could have. A better question is not so much could we have gone wrong, but did we? And that remains to be seen.

Given the collections from the Post Quarry and other Dockum localities, there may be as many as seven dinosaur species in the Texas Triassic. The fossils, however, are equivocal enough that there may be as few as two or three. Dinosaurs clearly do not appear to be the dominant members of the Dockum animal community. The dominant members were reptiles, to be sure, and even fairly closely related to dinosaurs, but they are different.

The top carnivore was a creature called *Postosuchus,* named for the Post Quarry by Chatterjee and originally proposed to have a special evolutionary relationship with much younger dinosaurs such as *Tyrannosaurus rex.* That relationship has now been discounted, but it is true that *Postosuchus* does resemble *T. rex* in some features. This is true not because they are especially close evolutionarily but because they evolved adaptations to their similar ways of life convergently. Both are top carnivores and they look like it. Their distant ancestors were different—not top carnivores—and did not look so much alike. The two evolutionary lineages evolved to resemble each other, but the ecological adaptations of their end members cannot mask their true relationships when examined in detail. The phenomenon of convergent evolution is more common than you might think whenever natural selection guides the evolution of species to a particular specialized way of life.

Postosuchus, over twelve feet long, was one of the largest animals on the Dockum landscape. The body was lightly built for its size, and according to Chatterjee, *Postosuchus* usually walked on its hind legs. The skull is close to two feet long. It is very narrow toward the snout but broad in the back, and the jaws are armed with sharp teeth. When viewed from the side, the upper jaw is convex down while the lower jaw is concave up, allowing the two to work like garden shears while the serrated teeth sliced through flesh. *Postosuchus* had keen vision and an acute sense of smell, which it used as it stalked its upland environment. As Chatterjee says, it may have hunted in packs. He refers to *Postosuchus* as the lord of the Triassic, suggesting that its presence and that of its kin suppressed the emergence of dinosaurs as rulers of the land during that period.

The largest of the herbivores known from the Texas Dockum was a strange, rhinoceroslike critter called *Placerias*. It had tusks on either side of a horny beak, and the head was broad. It was heavily built. *Placerias* was more a mammal than a reptile, extending as it does from the mammalian branch of the family tree. However, it has some features that are primitive along that branch. That is why it was previously placed with similar animals into a group that used to be called mammal-like reptiles. In fact, it is the last of the large mammal-like reptiles. A tiny reptile of this group was found at the Post Quarry and named *Pachygenelus milleri*. *Pachygenelus* was carnivorous and was related to similar species in South America and South Africa, an attestation to the continuity of Pangea. There have even been true mammals—as opposed to the mammal-like reptiles—found in the Dockum, although such animals are very rare and hard to come by. However, they do demonstrate conclusively that early mammals and early dinosaurs were contemporaries.

The most abundant of the herbivores on the Dockum scene are related to *Postosuchus* but were strange, bony-armored beasts with horns extending along the sides of the body in some of them. They are not dinosaurs but are related to them, just as crocodiles, as ruling reptiles or archosaurs, are. Their armor was made of bony plates in the skin, like crocodiles and alligators. Some of the plates are drawn out into a long, curved point, which is what makes the shoulder and side horns in *Desmatosuchus*. *Typothorax* is similar but lacks large horns. Those are just two members of this group of reptiles. There is an amazing diversity of these kinds of herbivores in the North American Triassic. All of the teeth known from them are simple and leaf-shaped, indicating a diet of soft vegetation. Another kind of reptile contemporary, the Dockum rhynchosaur, called *Otischalkia* after Otis Chalk in Howard County near Big Spring, was an odd, pig-sized herbivore with a strongly down-curved beak.

There are many lizardlike animals known from the Dockum, and these probably led lives similar to those of lizards today. Some are related to the modern tuatara of islands off the coast of New Zealand. Others had teeth that formed ridges running across the jaws. It is unclear just how many species

Postosuchus, *the top carnivore of the Dockum Triassic, heads to the water, watched by* Desmatosuchus, *an armored reptile with long shoulder spines. In the water are fish of various species.* Phytosaurs, *which superficially resembled crocodiles, were the major aquatic carnivores. The amphibians were like broad-headed fish traps. Illustration by Karen Carr.*

of lizardlike animals may have inhabited the Dockum because their fossils are so fragmentary. In addition, some had hollow, venom-conducting teeth known from the Triassic of North Carolina and from Arizona. I bet one day someone will find a venomous Triassic reptile in Texas, too.

Closer to the water's edge, the animals took on a different cast. The top carnivore was something that looks like a crocodile but is not. It is a phytosaur. This is a very clear example of convergent evolution. It is much less confusing than the possible case of *Shuvosaurus* discussed earlier because the skeletons of both crocodilians and phytosaurs are very well known. Phytosaurs have long snouts like crocodiles, but there is something very different. Crocodiles have nostrils at the end of their snouts. They also have a bony palate in their mouths that separates the air canals leading from the nostrils to the throat. This allows them to breathe while almost totally submerged, with only their nostrils above water level. Phytosaurs could also breathe while submerged in water, but for a different anatomical reason. Their nostrils are way back on the head, nearly between the eyes, and sit on a raised platform. When the animal breathed, air made a short trip down to its throat, bypassing the mouth. The opening of the raised nostrils on top of the head needed to be out, but the rest of the body could be hidden in the water.

Phytosaurs are also different from contemporary crocodiles and alligators because they have teeth that are flattened from side to side like knife blades instead of being rounded like cones. That is not a hard and fast rule for either group, however. Nevertheless, despite their being on very different branches of the evolutionary tree, phytosaurs look a lot like crocodiles and alligators in things other than their teeth and nostrils. They have long snouts, long bodies, long tails, short legs, and bones in the skin of their backs, and so do crocs and alligators. (That is why only the belly skin of crocodiles can be used for making leather if you like that sort of thing.) Phytosaurs probably shared with crocs and alligators a similar way of making a living, by lounging around the water's edge until an unwary land dweller got too close. They also probably ate fish and other aquatic fare, plus whatever else they could nab.

Fish are abundant in the Dockum and represent many different species. In fact, all Dockum fossil localities contain some aquatic elements. There are two kinds of small freshwater sharks. There are also bony fish with heavy scales related to gars. Some were streamlined, rapid swimmers while others were deep-bodied and slower. Some have sharp, needlelike teeth while others have crushing plates for eating mollusks. Then there is a lungfish, which would have burrowed into the mud during times of drought and slept through the hard times in a mucus cocoon. There is even a coelacanth, *Chinlea,* a relative of the living fossil now found in the waters near the Comoro Islands near

Triassic phytosaurs (bottom) *resemble modern alligators, which inhabit southeastern Texas today, but the resemblance is superficial. It is the consequence of evolutionary adaptation to similar ways of life, a phenomenon called convergent evolution. In the Triassic a phytosaur might lie next to a pond as a* Coelophysis *stands nearby. Nowadays, an alligator basks while a heron looks on. Illustration by Karen Carr.*

Madagascar. Coelacanths were thought to have been extinct for eighty million years until one turned up on a South African fishing trawler in 1938. Coelacanths and lungfish are important from an evolutionary perspective because knowledge of them is relevant to the origin of amphibians and the initial attainment of vertebrate life on land. This is so even though conquering life on land occurred long before the animals of the Dockum lived. Coelacanths and lungfish are a sister group with whom amphibians shared a close common ancestor from which they both evolved.

The amphibians around commonly in the Dockum were large, flat-headed labyrinthodonts, so called because the enamel of their teeth is infolded into a maze for extra strength. These were close in age to the last of the labyrinthodonts in North America, although the group as a whole appears to have persisted longer in China and Australia. They possessed absurd heads, broad and flat like a pancake spatula. The skull roof was solid, except for nostrils and holes for the eyes to bulge through. Sharp teeth lined the jaws. The limbs are almost ridiculously small, but the breast bones seem like skid plates. These amphibians were animated fish traps, lying in the bottom waters with their mouths open, waiting to snap shut and entrap a fish when its fins triggered the jaws to close. Above the water flew small pterosaurs. There may even have been some gliding reptiles. There were no birds—unless *Protoavis* proves to be one.

So you see, the life of the Dockum was extremely varied. Dinosaurs were only a small part of it. They were minor elements in the ecological web of the time, at least for most of it. Like all ecological webs, that of Dockum times relies ultimately on plants. No animal can live without plants. That is obviously true for herbivores because they must eat plants to live, but it is also true for animals that never eat plants. First and foremost, plants produce oxygen as a byproduct of photosynthesis as they convert the energy of sunlight into sugar and starch. No air-breathing animal could live without plants. Given that basic fact, it then becomes important that plants are a food source—the most basic food source—for animals, at the very foundation of the ecological pyramid. They are primary producers. All animal food is derived from plants, either directly or through a number of intermediate steps. Herbivores eat plants; carnivores eat herbivores.

Plants of the Dockum would seem depleted by today's standards because flowering plants had not yet evolved. The trees were all gymnosperms, or naked-seed plants, so named because their seeds are not protected in a special covering. You can see for yourself the next time you look at a pine cone and notice how the scales of the cone open to expose the seeds. That is very different from, say, an apple, which is a flowering plant and has its seeds deeply protected. Much of the understory and ground cover below the trees comprised ferns, scouring rushes, and cycads.

The diversity of the vertebrate life in the Dockum; the strange, archaic creatures mingled with the more familiar (albeit primitive) members of still-living groups; and the odd place of dinosaurs in the community show the Triassic Period to be a very interesting time in vertebrate evolution. We are fortunate to have such a good record of it in Texas.

Let us be clear about why the Triassic is such an important interval in vertebrate history. First, it is a time of phenomenal transitions in the cast of characters in the continuing ecological and evolutionary play of vertebrates. Most of the members that dominate the community are remnants of groups that were approaching the end of their evolutionary history. The big, flat-headed amphibians were nearing the end of their range in North America. So were most of the archaic lizard-sized reptiles, the gliding reptiles, some of the aquatic reptiles, and the big armored reptiles. At the same time, more familiar groups were unobtrusively entering the scene. What was beginning in the Triassic is of supreme importance to us because it includes the ancestors from which emerged the obvious animal life that exists today.

What would we not have now if things had not happened as they did in the Triassic? We would not have alligators basking in the marshes of the southeastern part of the state. Crocodiles and alligators trace their origins as a group back to the Triassic. We would not have snakes, lizards, and tuataras, those lizardlike reptiles now confined to islands off the coast of New Zealand. These groups share a common origin in the Triassic. We would not know of any of the dinosaurs, but more relevant to our modern life, we would have no birds. No sea gulls, no condors, no sparrows, no parakeets—none of them. They all trace their origins through twists and turns of a gnarly tree of life back to the origins of the dinosaurs in the Triassic. And we would have no mammals. That means we would not be here because main-line mammals have their origin in the Triassic, too. It was quite a time.

What caused the extinctions of the more archaic members of the Triassic fauna—extinctions which perhaps even contributed to the dinosaur dominance of the land? Why were some evolutionary lineages, including the dinosaurs, able to carry on after the extinctions? That is a good question, as it is for all extinction events. And there is no doubt that the Triassic Period ended with a significant extinction event. Maybe it was caused by climate. After the Triassic, global climates seem to have become more arid. But the story has to be more complex. Recall that the Dockum represents a sweep of time millions of years long. Life on Earth was not static during that interval. Things were changing throughout the Dockum era. Different portions of it were characterized by different suites of species. It has even been suggested that instead of one big extinction at the end of the Triassic, there may actually have been two extinction events closely spaced toward the end of the period.

It is possible that one or even more extinction events occurred during Dockum time before the end of the Triassic. Maybe extinction opened the landscape for dinosaurs. Perhaps it was only after one particular extinction event that dinosaurs are found in such abundance at Ghost Ranch, and possibly such diversity at the Post Quarry. After that not-quite-the-end Triassic extinction event, ecological communities adjusted and reorganized, allowing dinosaurs to gain a stronger foothold toward gaining a dominant place in the Mesozoic world.

What would have caused this extinction? Here we have an interesting phenomenon. Ever since the terminal Cretaceous extinctions were said to have been caused by a meteoric impact, a subject we will return to in the final chapter, the search has been on to find similar cases in Earth history. Maybe this is one. There is a crater, the Manicouagan crater, in Quebec that is about the right age, approximately 214 million years old. Perhaps that impact caused extinction of archaic reptiles and thus opened the door for dinosaurs. Then, 208 million years ago, at the end of the Triassic, perhaps there was another extinction, this one more related to climatic change than to extraterrestrial happenings. It remains to be seen.

The Triassic of Texas shows us the recurrent theme of Earth history, and that is change. Something is always changing because the Earth is dynamic. Different organisms respond in their own ways to change. Some evolve new forms, some go extinct, and for some the changes are not great enough to matter, at least at the time. But there is a cumulative effect, so when we view the Earth from one time period to the next, it is not the same. Pangea was the original homestead, but only for a while, and even while it was, internal forces were breaking it apart, and life was evolving in ways that set the stage for the next world.

CHAPTER 3

The Heart of Texas Dinosaurs

THE SECOND WORLD OF TEXAS DINOSAURS is not at all like the first. The dinosaurs are not the same, the geography is not the same, almost nothing is the same. It is a different world. This world of Texas dinosaurs began 119 million years ago and ended at 95 million, so it falls smack in the middle of the Cretaceous Period. Its location is deep in the very heart of Texas.

The supercontinent of Pangea that characterized the first world of Texas dinosaurs was long disintegrated. The North American continent was better defined as its own land mass, although it did not look exactly as it does today. To the south, there was no Isthmus of Panama. North and South America were completely separated by ocean waters. On the other hand, South America was only then beginning its final separation from Africa. The northern Atlantic was a good, wide ocean, while the southern Atlantic was poised to open. This would allow the waters of the south to mix with those of the north, establishing a new pattern of oceanic circulation.

At the time the second world of Texas dinosaurs began, the heart of Texas was at the coast of what we can think of as the ancient Gulf of Mexico. Sea level was higher then, and the waters of the proto-gulf extended much farther north. All of the coastal and near-coastal area of present-day Texas, including the locations of Houston, Galveston, Corpus

Acrocanthosaurus, *the terror of the Early Cretaceous, eyes a small mammal. Illustration by Karen Carr, courtesy Fort Worth Museum of Science and History.*

Christi, and even Huntsville and beyond, was underwater.

The seas of this world were not still. They rose and fell often over the course of the twenty-four million years that comprise the geologic time interval of the second world, a global seiche on a grand temporal scale. The rising and falling of sea level means that the coastline was continuously changing: sometimes lying near Waco, at other times closer to Gainesville, and often somewhere in between. As we now look at the rocks of Central and northern Texas, we see the results of a migrating coastline reflected in the kinds of rocks that occur, stacked one layer upon another. Rocks deposited in marine settings, such as in the deep sea or on carbonate platforms, display recognizable characteristics that allow us to interpret the environment of deposition and, thereby, to reconstruct ancient environments and geographies. Near shore rocks formed from sediments along beaches, tidal flats, or lagoons have their own recognizable characteristics, too. Basically, all that is needed to figure out the positions of the ancient migrating coastline are a good geologic map and some measured sections of the rock units. Robert T. Hill's greatest con-

Philip Hobson (center), *his son, Brian, and Arnold Palmer of SMU* (left) *watch as a block of stone is hoisted from the creek bed. This is how the* Acrocanthosaurus *skeleton was removed. Photograph by Dennis E. Gabbard, courtesy Fort Worth Museum of Science and History.*

tribution to the geological sciences was in mapping near-shore rocks in north-central Texas, the region he called the Black and Grand Prairies. Because of such fieldwork, we can actually trace through the rocks the shifting of the coastline through time.

It is particularly interesting for us that near-shore rocks, whether on the ocean side or the land side, are very good at preserving fossils. Of course, marine rocks overwhelmingly contain the fossils of animals that lived in the sea. Occasionally, however, land-dwelling vertebrates like dinosaurs get washed out into the salt water, where they are buried along with the bodies of marine organisms. Moreover, the oceans of the Earth are vast, and many sea creatures have a broad geographic range. Because they inhabit tremendously large areas of the Earth, the fossils of marine organisms are extremely important in correlating the ages of rocks from place to place and thus in telling geologic time. Therefore, any dinosaurs that are washed into the sea can be dated by the associated invertebrates and microfossils of the marine realm.

Even more importantly, the transgressions of the sea over land and the regression of receding shorelines result in sequences of terrestrial sediments packaged stratigraphically between marine rocks and the erosional surfaces produced by fluctuations in sea level. Why should that be important? Because in many cases, the rise or fall of sea level is a global phenomenon. Therefore, we are aided in the correlation of what was happening in Central Texas with what might have been going on elsewhere on the Earth at the same time. For all these reasons, we end up with a well-dated sequence of dinosaurs in north-central Texas, where there are either no rocks suitable for radiometric age determination or those that are have not been aggressively subjected to the process.

The second world of Texas dinosaurs is actually fairly widespread across the state. The reason is because much of what is now the southern three-quarters of Texas was a flat shelf area bordered by a deeper ocean, over which the sea could easily roll with a slight increase in water depth or recede with shallowing. Scrappy bones of Cretaceous dinosaurs have been found in the Quitman Mountains along the Rio Grande south of El Paso and out toward Big Bend. Most bones, however, are concentrated more in the north-central region of the state from Irion County west of San Angelo to the Dallas–Fort Worth International Airport, and from north of the Red River in Oklahoma south through Wise and Montague counties east of Decatur. The appropriate rocks continue in a band to the southwest, over to Tarrant County west of Fort Worth and to Parker County around Weatherford. They then reach farther south to the area around Granbury in Hood County, Glen Rose in Somervell County, Stephenville in Erath County, and Proctor in Comanche

County. They extend beyond those counties in the Brazos River drainage and the Lampasas Cut Plain and continue to near Austin, circling around Marble Falls and the eastern, southern, and western margins of the Llano Uplift. Suitable rocks crop out sporadically around much of the Edwards Plateau. However, most of the best fossils come from within about one hundred miles of Dallas and Fort Worth.

This area, especially the northern part of it, is rich in a variety of fossils. It has produced as many as ten species of dinosaurs: some that are just now in the process of being named, others that remain to be studied. This richness of dinosaurs is significant because it falls at a time in Earth history when little is known of dinosaurs and their neighbors yet it is extremely important for the emergence of the modern world with which we are so familiar. In many ways, the clues to the history of life provided by the dinosaurs and other fossils in the second world bestow a significance that makes this the heart of the Texas dinosaur story.

The incursions and regressions of the sea allow us to break the twenty-four-million-year story of the heart of Texas dinosaurs into manageable sequences of dinosaur-bearing rocks separated by marine rocks that lack dinosaurs, although they have lots of other interesting, mainly invertebrate, critters. Dinosaurs occur in three intervals in north-central Texas. We will proceed, as geologists and paleontologists do, from oldest to youngest.

The first set of dinosaur strata is of the longest duration and is the most complex. It begins close to 119 million years ago, when, for the first time, terrestrial rocks of the Cretaceous Period were deposited in north-central Texas. It is complicated because during the middle of it there was an incursion of the sea that divided the terrestrial strata into a lower Twin Mountains and an upper Paluxy Formation. Between the two lies the Glen Rose Limestone, representing the shallow sea and its tidal flats. This arrangement is easily observed west of Weatherford in Parker County, south to the vicinity of Stephenville and Proctor in Erath and Comanche counties, and along the Paluxy River in Hood and Somervell counties. However, going north, about when you arrive at Paradise in Wise County, the Glen Rose pinches out, because the sea did not transgress farther north. The Twin Mountains and Paluxy merge into one rock unit, now called the Antlers Formation. Without the marine rocks of the Glen Rose to divide the sequence into smaller sections, it is harder to nail down the ages of the terrestrial fossils. Therefore, we have better time control on the Twin Mountains, Glen Rose, and Paluxy formations than we do on the Antlers.

As you might guess, it is in the Glen Rose Formation, near that town, where the famous dinosaur tracks are found, including those that Bird and his crews excavated. The main track layer at Dinosaur Valley State Park is estimated to be 111 million years old. Glen Rose rocks with dinosaur tracks are found over much of Central and West Texas, but the tracks from along the Paluxy have been studied the most and are the best known. The tracks are found in what was once muddy tidal flats on the edge of the Glen Rose sea.

As the sea eventually retreated, the land dried out and terrestrial depositional conditions resumed. That is when the Paluxy and the upper part of the Antlers formations were deposited. Resting on top of the Paluxy and Antlers is a marine unit called the Walnut Formation, deposited when the sea rose once more, putting an end to terrestrial sedimentation and the oldest set of dinosaurs from the heart of Texas. The base of the Walnut Formation is estimated to be 105 million years old. Thus, the first installment of the heart of Texas dinosaurs embraces the 14-million-year stretch between 119 and 105 million years ago. That interval of terrestrial sedimentation is broken up in part of its range by the incursion of the Glen Rose sea, in which were deposited the rocks of the Glen Rose Formation.

At least six distinct species of dinosaurs are known from the interval composed of the Twin Mountains, Glen Rose, and Paluxy formations. Three of them are herbivorous, bird-hipped ornithischians and three are lizard-hipped saurischians, one herbivorous and the other two carnivorous.

The smallest of the herbivores is a new species, not yet described. It belongs to a large group of small ornithischians called hypsilophodonts (HIP-suh-LOH-fuh-dont). Representatives of the group are known from England, South America, Africa, Australia, and even Antarctica. They have been known to occur in north-central Texas for thirty years or so. But it was not until 1985, when Rusty Branch, a student at Tarleton State University, found bone at Proctor Lake in Comanche County, that Texas hypsilophodonts came to center stage. Rusty, who is now a paleontology graduate student at Baylor University, made one of the greatest finds in Texas dinosaur history. He did not find just a few teeth, which was what was known previously. He found skeletons, and a lot of them. Can you imagine what Rusty felt like when he saw what was before him?

The hypsilophodonts that Rusty found grew to be about ten feet long from snout to tail. Their hands had five fingers, but the pinky was just a stub. Their front limbs were shorter than their hind limbs. There were four toes on the foot, with the inside toe shorter than the rest. While foraging slowly, they might walk about on all fours. For faster running, they went to two feet. Their faces were short and deep. Their cheek teeth formed a continuous sharp ridge in each jaw for slicing up vegetation. Small teeth lay toward the front of the mouth, but a horny beak covered the tip.

Little hypsilophodonts drink, not yet fully aware of the Deinonychus, *which has them in view. Illustration by Karen Carr, courtesy Fort Worth Museum of Science and History.*

Hypsilophodonts were probably active little herbivores, sort of like the dinosaur equivalent of gazelles. They probably formed flocks and bounded from plant to plant, plucking the tender leaves and shoots. They had little with which to defend themselves except the watchful eyes of the flock, which kept a lookout for predators, and a quick and sprightly gait with which to escape.

Rusty found more than a bunch of bones at Proctor Lake. He found a unique locality in the Texas Cretaceous. The site is a stretch of red sedimentary rocks extending for a half-mile. Within this stretch of red rocks is a band of strata about six feet thick dotted with more than sixty concentrations of hypsilophodont bones. Rusty found the richest concentration of dinosaur bones in the state!

Everything about the Proctor Lake site is interesting. First of all, red sedimentary rocks like those at Proctor Lake are rare in the Twin Mountains Formation, the rock unit that contains the site. They represent muds that were deposited on ancient floodplains along rivers flowing southeastward to the sea, whose shore lay some fifty to one hundred miles distant. Plants grew

Rusty Branch at Proctor Lake. He discovered the richest dinosaur site in Texas while he was an undergraduate at Tarleton State University. He is now a graduate student at Baylor. Courtesy of James R. Branch.

and soils developed on the floodplain muds. The action of plant roots eventually bleached light green halos around themselves in the red dirt, resulting in a mottled color pattern in the rocks we see today. Calcium carbonate precipitated from waters percolating through the ground to form caliche nodules. The climate was warm, semiarid, and distinctly seasonal. That was the environment in which the Texas hypsilophodont lived. This environment must have remained relatively stable for thousands—perhaps tens of thousands—of years because the hypsilophodont fossils are not uniformly spread through the site. Instead, they are found in discrete areas dotted through the six-foot-thick section of rock along its quarter-mile outcrop.

Some of the spots at Proctor Lake where fossils are found contain only a bone or two. Most places contain more. The bones from Proctor Lake represent both young and adult individuals. Often the adults are found as nearly complete skeletons, with the bones articulated and still joined together as in life. Their necks are often arched back and their legs drawn up, indicating that their tissues dried and shrank before burial. Surprisingly, there are many fewer adults than there are young hypsilophodonts at Proctor Lake.

The young occur in a completely different context from most of the adults. They are hardly ever found alone as isolated individuals. Almost always they occur with others of a similarly small size, more or less in a jumbled mass—sometimes with the remains of more than ten dinosaurs in one spot. Only parts of the skeletons remain articulated. These concentrations of bone lie in small depressions on the old land surface. Such a jumble of bones from a number of individuals is sort of like having several chickens in the same stew pot: some parts of each skeleton hang together, but the rest of the bones get mixed up.

None of the specimens, adult or juvenile, shows signs of extensive scavenging. In fact, although most of the bones are cracked and sometimes distorted from the ordeal of being buried in soft sediments for more than 100 million years, some of them show a distinctive surface texture that indicates they lay in the sun and the elements on top of the ground for some time before they were finally buried. This kind of treatment produces a recognizable pattern of cracking on the surface of the bones, which is observed at Proctor Lake. Thus, after death the carcasses were exposed to drying and degradation before being interred. However, none of the bones seemed to have been aligned by flowing water, so the carcasses were not concentrated by a flash flood. They were buried as they lay when the ancient river spilled through its bank and dropped mud from its splaying waters. The only other fossils besides the hypsilophodonts at Proctor Lake are those of a small crocodile and one tooth of a meat-eating theropod.

What a strange fossil locality! So many young, yet so few adults, and not much of anything except hypsilophodont dinosaurs, which are otherwise extremely rare in the Texas Cretaceous. The behavior of these animals must have played a role in forming the concentration of bones at Proctor Lake. Why else would young of the same size be massed together in shallow depressions? Why would so many hypsilophodont skeletons be together at all if not for their behavior? We know that their bodies were not brought together by the action of the river that deposited the sediments entombing the fossils. If that were the case, the river would have rearranged the bones.

The first possibility that comes to mind is that maybe Proctor Lake was an old nesting ground for hypsilophodonts, protected from most predators and a safe haven for a nest. That may be the case, but where are the egg shells? Perhaps eons of groundwater percolating through the strata have dissolved them away. Maybe the shells were destroyed in the process of soil formation, chemically broken down by plant roots and the chemical environment of the earth.

Most of the hypsilophodonts at Proctor Lake are small, and therefore they were younger individuals than the larger specimens. In any given concentration of small bones at Proctor Lake, the animals that make it up tend to be of similar size. However, from concentration to concentration the size of bones varies. Although all of the concentrations contain young animals, some are composed of slightly larger, and therefore slightly older, young individuals. That means that not all of the young were newly hatched, no matter where the nests might have been.

Some species of ground-dwelling birds lead their young away from the nest site soon after hatching. This is presumably to avoid the danger of predators who might detect them through the litter of the nest or simply by staying in one place for too long. Birds must often leave the nest area to forage. Indeed, the ends of the limb bones of even the smallest Proctor Lake hypsilophodont are well formed, indicating that this species was precocious and could run about soon after hatching. This is similar to some species of modern birds, like quail; or, better yet, the flightless emus, rheas, and ostriches.

The largest of the living flightless birds is the ostrich. It looks like what we might imagine a feathery, traditional dinosaur would look like, although it has only two toes on its feet. However deceiving the comparison of ostriches and dinosaurs might be considering the differences between modern birds and Mesozoic denizens, the ostrich has a particularly informative, interesting, and probably relevant life history with respect to the Proctor Lake hypsilophodont. The ostrich is an egg-laying, active, bipedal species, not endowed with exceptional ferocity and too large to be consistently inconspicuous. Many dinosaur species have those traits. The Proctor Lake hypsilophodont shares them, although the ostrich is a larger animal.

Ostriches have a strange kind of mating system where several females lay eggs in one nest, but only one dominant pair broods the eggs. Immediately after hatching, the chicks are active and ready to forage. In their quest for food, the chicks, watched over by the dominant male and female, roam the plains. Sooner or later they meet another flock. After the encounter, the baby-sitting duties often fall to one pair of adults, with the other pair being dismissed and run off. After a while the chicks of several nests band together in a large group, or crèche, sometimes with well over a hundred young ostriches, all overseen by just a few adults. The banding together of so many young into one group presumably increases the odds of survival for them all. For example, if a jackal were to make a meal of one chick from a group of four, the odds are one in four, or 25 percent, that any given chick will be eaten. If the jackal is stalking a crèche of one hundred and fifty chicks, the odds of any given chick being eaten are considerably less.

Perhaps the fossil accumulation at Proctor Lake is reflecting a similar behavior for hypsilophodonts. That would explain an abundance of young with only a few adults. However, it is extremely difficult to prove that we are really dealing with a dinosaurian crèche because, you will recall, the Proctor Lake locality was formed over a period of thousands of years. But even if hypsilophodont behavior was not like ostriches, there are nevertheless clusters of young animals together that need to be explained. It may be that Proctor Lake represents a foraging area, consistently visited over time by coveys of dinosaurs, with the occasional family group meeting its end in that area two or three times every thousand years.

What could have caused this local demise of hypsilophodonts at Proctor Lake? Who knows. Because the deposit formed over time, it was not just one event—it must have been a series of them. It was not flash floods, judging from the geological occurrence of the bones. Perhaps drought played a role: after all, the climate was seasonal. Perhaps disease, such as the duck plague that occurs now in Texas, played a role. The agent of death may have been one factor that recurred periodically. It may have been something as understandable as late freezes, cold snaps that caught the beasts at particularly vulnerable times in their life histories. There is still much to learn. In general, however, it can be said that the fossil deposit at Proctor Lake represents what is left of a series of generations of one hypsilophodont species that inhabited the region for a short interval between 119 and 113 million years ago. The period during which the entire Proctor Lake sample was formed was a rather short interval of geologic time, on the order of thousands to a few tens of thousands of years. That seems like a pretty long time to casually throw about, but it is a relatively small proportion of the time represented by the Twin Mountains Formation. The environmental conditions seem to have been stable during the interval that hypsilophodonts roamed the area. Each concentration of bones at Proctor Lake was probably derived from a single family group or some other biological aggregate. That is why the Dallas Museum of Natural History is placing three of the skeletons prepared in my lab on display, mounted as a family group.

No matter how the Proctor Lake locality was formed, the hypsilophodonts were important elements of the Early Cretaceous dinosaur community. They were widespread across Texas, from the Rio Grande to Forestburg. But nowhere else has this species been found in such abundance as at Proctor Lake. There was something special about the place.

During their heyday the hypsilophodonts were low on the food chain, the herbivorous prey of dinosaurian carnivores. Some of the young may have been taken by small crocodiles, like the ones found with them at Proctor Lake. When the young had matured sufficiently, they likely gathered with adults into flocks similar to gazelles, and probably for the same reasons: herds have more eyes and ears to sense danger, and, as discussed above, their numbers increase the odds of survival for each individual. These groups inhabited wooded valleys separated by intervening low divides. Through the valleys flowed streams that drained the flat countryside on their way to the sea.

But the sea was not far away, and sea level changed many times during the second world of the Texas dinosaurs. With all the comings and goings of the sea—some extensive, some less so—it seems obvious that many depositional environments would be represented in the rock formations. And they are. Beaches, streams, floodplains, brackish estuaries, and many more environments are all embodied by sediments of the Twin Mountains Formation, long since turned to stone. With such a diversity of habitats, it makes sense that the fossil assemblages would vary from environment to environment. That is in fact what we see. And that, of course, is one of the things that makes Proctor Lake different. Other dinosaur remains in the heart of Texas are found in rocks formed from sediments laid down in different environments from that at Proctor, usually closer to the sea.

That brings us to the next Twin Mountains species, *Tenontosaurus dossi* (te-NON-tuh-SAWR-us DOSS-eye), a horse-sized ornithischian herbivore with a surprisingly horsy-looking face. I have some special feelings for this species. A complete skeleton of it was prepared in my lab at SMU and is now on display at the Fort Worth Museum of Science and History. That is the first complete dinosaur skeleton I have had anything to do with that has been placed before the public, which is one reason why it is special. I also like where it was found, the way it was found, and the owners of the land on which it was found.

Tenontosaurus is a lot like the Proctor Lake hypsilophodont in a number of ways. But at greater than twenty feet in length (including the tail) and perhaps approaching a ton in weight, it is more than twice as long and well over eight times the weight of the largest Proctor Lake hypsilophodont. Nevertheless, *Tenontosaurus* has often been considered a member of the hypsilophodont family. It has four toes on the hind foot and five on the front. The little finger is short and splayed out. The front limbs are strong but shorter than the hind limbs. Like the Proctor Lake hypsilophodont, it probably walked about on all fours as it foraged, resorting to two legs during fast flight.

The name *Tenontosaurus* means "sinew lizard." It was chosen because ornithopod dinosaurs often have bony, ossified tendons running along the vertebrae of the tail, holding it stiff. With the tail cantilevered as a balance behind the animal, it offset the weight of the forequarters and head held out in front of the hips. In *Tenontosaurus* these ossified tendons are particularly impressive, lying both above and below the tail vertebrae. Nevertheless, they are similar to those in the Proctor Lake hypsilophodont. The first discovery of *Tenontosaurus* was in Montana. The complete name of the Montana species is *Tenontosaurus tilletti*. The genus has been known in Texas for thirty years,

Tenontosaurus dossi *being viewed by Joanna and Ralph, the daughter and husband of Karen Carr, the artist for this book, at Fort Worth Museum of Science and History. Illustration by Karen Carr.*

but for all that time it was not anywhere near close to being adequately studied.

Then, in 1988, seven-year-old Thad Williams and his father, Ted, a biology teacher at Millsap High School, were walking down a creek bed in Parker County. The stream was Lick Branch, which drains into Grindstone Creek. This is the same area where Robert T. Hill found the first Texas dinosaurs, but Thad and Ted did not know that at the time. They were just out walking. As it is with all boys and their fathers when they go out exploring, the son made a discovery. And this time, it was a real one that every kid wishes he could make. Thad and his father knelt beside a skull. It was long with a broad muzzle, like a horse. But they live in the country. They knew a horse when they saw one, even just the skull, and this was not a horse.

They took their find to Jim Diffily of the Fort Worth Museum of Science and History, who called my lab. The landowners, James and Dorothy Doss, gave the go-ahead to the Fort Worth museum to excavate and donated the

Tenontosaurus dossi
feeding and hypsilo-
phodonts pronking. Illus-
tration by Karen Carr.

bones to the museum. The bones were heavily encased in limy sandstone because the carcass had been washed into the sea. Oysters grew abundantly, encrusting the hard surface of the bones. The problem was to extricate the bones from their hard matrix without doing them damage. Jim brought them to my labs, and that is where they were prepared. It turns out there were really two individuals of *Tenontosaurus* at Doss Ranch, not just one as we originally thought. Now we know that they belong to a new species of Texas dinosaur. My colleagues Dale Winkler and Phil Murry and I are naming it *Tenontosaurus dossi*. It is more primitive than *Tenontosaurus tilletti* because it has little teeth at the front of the jaw, whereas *T. tilletti* does not, and for a few other anatomical reasons. After the bones were prepared and the study well under way, they were shipped to Arnie Lewis, formerly of Harvard and the Smithsonian, now retired in Florida. He built the armature, readied the bones for display, and brought them back to Fort Worth. Now you can go see the mounted skeleton at the museum any time you want. It is a very pleasing story of paleontological cooperation.

Tenontosaurus dossi is from the Twin Mountains Formation, the same rock unit that gave us the Proctor Lake hypsilophodont. Above the Twin Mountains Formation lies the Glen Rose, and above that the Paluxy. Interestingly enough, not much more than a mile west of the Doss ranch, Gary Spaulding, also a schoolteacher, discovered another dinosaur. This one was not in the Twin Mountains but from a younger formation. It was a *Tenontosaurus,* all right, but not *T. dossi.* It appears to be like *Tenontosaurus tilletti,* the more advanced species, first known from Montana but also long known from this area. Here in the heart of Texas, in one small area, with the rocks stacked like a layer cake, we can see the older, more primitive *T. dossi* in the Twin Mountains Formation and the younger, more derived *T. tilletti* in the overlying formations. It is indeed rare to find dinosaur evolution laid out so neatly.

The Doss Ranch dinosaur locality is quite unlike Proctor Lake, even though both fall technically within the same rock formation. The Doss Ranch site is more complicated in some respects. It was formed when a number of *Tenontosaurus dossi* individuals died on land, near the sea. They were then washed downstream and into brackish water to be buried. Oyster-rich limy sandstone encrusted the bones. Above the bones, the sediments were deposited in a low and swampy delta environment. Those sediments now form a stratum that is dark with the coalified remains of plants.

James and Dorothy Doss did much more for Texas dinosaur lovers than simply make the fossils from their land available for study and display. They also held a barbecue. All Texans love a barbecue, and to this one came the

Tenontosaurus *with* Pleurocoelus *in the background. Illustration by Karen Carr, courtesy Fort Worth Museum of Science and History.*

Seven-year-old Thad Williams with Ted, his dad, at the site where they discovered a new species of dinosaur, Tenontosaurus dossi. *Courtesy of Debbie Williams.*

The Pleurocoelus *locality at Jones Ranch. Billy Jones is in the dark cap* (center). *The crew is from SMU, the Fort Worth Museum of Science and History, Tarleton State University, East Texas State University, and Baylor University. Photograph by Donald Garland, courtesy of Fort Worth Museum of Science and History.*

Dosses' neighboring landowners. After a friendly feed, James Doss stood before his neighbors and made an announcement.

"You all know about the dinosaur," he said. "These folks are from SMU, and they have been working on it. They go on my land. They don't scare the cows and they close all the gates. You might think, if you want to, about letting them go on your land to look for dinosaurs."

As we stood around talking afterwards, a tall fellow in a cowboy hat sidled up.

"I have a dinosaur on my land. Why don't you come have a look at it?"

Philip Hobson owns the land just over the hill from the Doss place. The same rock strata are exposed on either side of the hill. The land used to belong to Philip's grandfather. He remembers as a child playing along the creek on the big rocks that jutted from the bank. In the rocks, he said, were bones. Hobson spoke of teeth sticking out in a row. He said his grandfather had taken a piece of the stone with fossil bone in it to Fort Worth forty years earlier, but nothing had come of it.

Reports this detailed, surprisingly enough, come in fairly often. I wanted to check it out, but after having checked out so many leads in the past that turned out to be things other than fossils, I reserved judgment until I saw it with my own eyes.

It did not take my own eyes long to know that what Philip had was a nearly complete skeleton of a large meat-eating dinosaur. The bones were mostly concealed in hard rock. The rock is the reason the bones were there and not weathered out and eroded away years ago. It protected the bone. More than that, these rocks formed because the bones were there. The dinosaur carcass originally came to rest on a sandbar in an ancient river flowing toward the sea. The carcass was covered with sand as the layers of earth built up. The flesh rotted and decomposed, changing the chemistry of the ground around the bones, making it different from the surrounding volume of sediments. Calcium carbonate lime came out of solution in the groundwater and cemented the sand around the skeletons inside rounded concretions that weigh several tons each. Those are the rocks that now protect the bone.

And there it was when Philip showed it to me. Four huge concretions, laid out like a jigsaw puzzle. Most of the bones were hidden inside the concretions, but enough was showing that we knew what we had. That is just about, but not quite, the same situation we are in to this day. The problem is that the concretions containing the bones are so hard that it takes diamond blades and lots of time to extricate the fossils from their dense matrix. But we have made progress. To get the bones out of the ground in the first place, the crew from SMU, the Fort Worth Museum of Science and History, and

Tarleton State dug around the multi-ton concretions. We split some of them to make them more manageable, then jacked them up with house jacks. Once the concretions were off the ground, we slid railroad ties underneath to hold them up. Then came the crane from F. B. McIntire Equipment Co. out of Fort Worth. We slipped straps alongside the railroad ties under the blocks and hoisted the heavy concretions with their bony treasure out of the creek channel and onto the bank.

As I write this, three blocks—about half what we started with—are decorating Mr. Hobson's lawn. I can only handle one big one in my lab at a time, and the concretions are hard, so it is slow going. Thus far, we have extracted both thigh bones, part of the hip, several vertebrae, a few ribs, and some fragmentary skull bones. I am not discouraged. The progress we have made in the past year and a half is quite substantial. Each day brings new bone to light, new minidiscoveries about a creature long extinct. The process takes time. And besides, if these Texas dinosaurs were easy—and especially if the Hobson theropod were—they would have been done already! All of us involved in this project can see down the road to when the Hobson theropod will be mounted in Fort Worth, next to *Tenontosaurus dossi,* exhibited for everyone to see.

Even given the state of preparation now, we know some interesting things about the Hobson theropod. We know that much of the skeleton is present, making this the only reasonably complete large meat-eating dinosaur specimen known from Texas. The thigh bone is over a meter long, indicating that the total length of this animal when mounted will be over thirty feet. From what can be seen of the vertebrae, the creature looks similar to a dinosaur from the Antlers Formation in Oklahoma called *Acrocanthosaurus atokensis* (ACK-roh-KAN-thuh-SAWR-us AY-toh-KEN-sis). I do not know if it is the same species, or even the same genus, and I will not until the Hobson specimen is fully prepared from the rock and studied in detail. Nevertheless, *Acrocanthosaurus* was a big meat eater with long spines sticking up from the vertebrae. This suggests that it had either a sail or a large hump, like a buffalo, running along its back.

The Hobson theropod lived at the same time and in the same area as *Tenontosaurus dossi.* Like most meat eaters, this theropod probably ate whatever it could catch or scavenge. Because it was so large, it could take large prey, perhaps *Tenontosaurus.* A hypsilophodont would have made a tasty morsel. However, the real giant around here was the brontosaur *Pleurocoelus.* From the trackways collected at Glen Rose and now in the American Museum of Natural History in New York, Roland T. Bird, as we saw in chapter 1, could imagine the attack of a carnivore like the Hobson theropod on the behemoth *Pleurocoelus.*

There is more to that story of sauropod and theropod footprints, however. Bird's vision was based on a set of trackways in which theropod tracks paralleled those of a sauropod. Near where the trackways overlap, one of the theropod tracks is missing, as if an attack occurred and the carnivore was lifted off the ground, carried along by the larger but agonizing victim. The overlapping of the tracks creates the potential problem of the sauropod's tail being in the way of the attack on its flank. An alternative interpretation to the one-on-one attack is that a pack of theropods followed after the sauropod, perhaps stalking it or perhaps not. It is impossible to say for sure. There is no smoking gun. Nevertheless, even if the trackway does not show an actual stalking, *Pleurocoelus* surely had natural enemies, at least when young, and large theropods like *Acrocanthosaurus* and the Hobson specimen fit that bill.

It has also been suggested that sauropod footprints in Texas indicate gregarious behavior, perhaps even showing that the young congregated on the interior of the herd. Evidence for that interpretation is inconclusive, but it does seem likely that *Pleurocoelus* formed groups. It remains to be determined with certainty what the structure of the groups was. However, parental care among dinosaurs is well documented for several other species, so it would not be unreasonable to expect that parental care and protection might be manifested in sauropod herd structure.

Footprints at Glen Rose can appear confusing for another reason. Bones are given names just as if they are real living species. Footprints are given a separate set of names. In this case, the sauropod footprints in the Glen Rose Formation are called *Brontopodus birdi* (BRONT-uh-POHD-us BIRD-eye), and the theropod tracks have been called *Irenesauripus glenrosensis* (EYE-rene-SAWR-uhp-us GLEN-ROSE-ENS-is). Nevertheless, regardless of the two sets of names, we have a good idea of what made the tracks. The *Irenesauripus glenrosensis* footprints have long been attributed to *Acrocanthosaurus* or something like it. Teeth and a few bones of other species of small theropods are known from the Twin Mountains, Paluxy, and Antlers formations, but none of their tracks can be confidently identified. These rocks are the right age to have raptors like *Deinonychus* (dye-NON-ick-us) within them, and some of the incomplete material may actually belong to it, but no tracks of *Deinonychus* or its relatives are known from Texas. They would be easy to identify because the tracks would show only two well-formed toes instead of three, as in clear theropod prints at Glen Rose. The third toe in *Deinonychus* supported an enlarged, slashing claw.

Brontopodus tracks are clearly the footprints of *Pleurocoelus* because *Brontopodus* designates the tracks of a large, quadrupedal sauropod. *Pleurocoelus* bones are found nearby. Rare, large ornithopod tracks, thought to have been made by a bipedal iguanodont, are found in similar age rocks but not at Dinosaur Valley State Park. There are a few bones in the area that show an ornithopod, probably an iguanodont, larger than *Tenontosaurus* was here. There are occasional small footprints around that could have been made by a hypsilophodont. However, there are no prints known that seem likely to have been made by *Tenontosaurus*. That is because Tenontosaurus is a medium-sized ornithopod with a relatively long internal toe, suggesting that its tracks would leave the impression of four toes at least part of the time, depending on the surface on which it was walking.

There is one other thing that is not present anywhere dinosaur footprints are found: human tracks. Those who would claim that the footprints of humans are found preserved in stone with those of dinosaurs are expressing a world view, not a scientific observation. There are some elongate three-toed tracks at Glen Rose that are curious, not because of what made them—they are dinosaur tracks—but because of the reason they are elongate. The tracks are made long because a part of the foot that did not usually touch the ground while walking did so in these cases. Was the mud a different texture, causing that to happen? Were the dinosaurs behaving differently, perhaps dancing in display, while they made these tracks? We do not yet know.

What have we learned from the footprints at Glen Rose and other places in Texas? One of the most important things suggested by the abundance of trackways is that often the major track makers—both sauropod and theropod—were gregarious, preferring the company of others of their kind to being alone. Besides showing that dinosaurs often aggregated in the same areas, the footprints can provide clues to the speed at which dinosaurs were traveling. One theropod, for instance, was estimated to be moving twenty-five miles per hour, based on Texas footprints. The sauropods and most of the other theropods were traveling more slowly. Because there are no tail drags, all of the dinosaurs that left tracks were probably holding their tails off the ground. The depth of sauropod prints suggests that these animals did not require the buoyancy of water to move about, as was argued in Bird's day; rather, giants that they were, their legs were strong and pillarlike, moving them in elephantine gaits.

The footprints along the Paluxy River, and most other tracks for that matter, are preserved as they were made: as the muddy impression of a step, now turned to stone. However, along the Brazos River in some places where the Glen Rose Formation is eroding out, it is not the impressions of feet that are being found. Instead, the mud infillings of tracks have turned to stone and weathered out to look like giant dinosaur track-shaped cookies. The mud that filled the tracks originally is of Cretaceous age, and in some of the "cookies," fossil fish teeth from the Age of Dinosaurs are preserved.

Footprints and bones provide two different but complementary approaches to the study of dinosaurs and their ways of life. When work on the Hobson theropod is complete, we will in all probability have a much better understanding of the big carnivorous dinosaur, which is the most likely candidate to be the track maker that made the three-toed tracks along the Paluxy near Glen Rose. As for the sauropod tracks, bones of *Pleurocoelus* have been known from Hood County to the north of Glen Rose for decades, but there has never been an adequate study of them. There is one particularly important locality on land owned by Billy Jones. He made it available first to the University of Texas and then to a joint project involving SMU, the Fort Worth Museum of Science and History, Tarleton State University, and East Texas State University. The bones at Jones Ranch lie high in the Twin Mountains Formation, not far below its contact with the Glen Rose. Excavating them is the biggest dinosaur project ever undertaken in the heart of Texas. It is the biggest project because *Pleurocoelus* is the largest of the dinosaurs in this area; the site is a pile of bones from several individuals; and, what is more, the bones are in the same kind of hard, intractable rock as the Hobson theropod! I have to say it again: if it were easy, it would already have been done.

In the sequence of formations from the Twin Mountains to the Glen Rose to the Paluxy, and in the Antlers Formation (their northern and western correlative), many of the good dinosaur specimens known come from the Twin Mountains. The Glen Rose is mainly marine, but its beds that were deposited in mud flats produce an extensive array of footprints and some bones. The Paluxy has produced good dinosaurs, such as the *Tenontosaurus tilletti* found by Gary Spaulding, which shows there were at least some changes in the dinosaurs between Twin Mountains and Paluxy times.

When the sea submerged the Antlers and Paluxy formations, it put an end to dinosaurs in this area for 5 million years, from 105 million to around 100 million years ago. This was a particularly interesting time for North American geography because by 100 million years ago the transgression of the sea had created the Western Interior Seaway, inundating not only parts of Texas but also parts of New Mexico, Arizona, Colorado, Kansas, and several other states to join the Gulf of Mexico with the Arctic Ocean. North America was split in two. It stayed that way until very near the end of the Age of Dinosaurs, 66 million years ago.

Several formations were laid down in Central Texas during the interval of marine transgression that culminated in the Western Interior Seaway. At about the time of its completion and just after, between 100 million and 97 million years ago (97.5 to be more exact), the sea along the eastern Texas shore shallowed. Under these conditions the Paw Paw Formation was deposited, and in it some truly astounding dinosaur discoveries have been made.

In 1989, when twelve-year-old Johnny Maurice showed the bones he found to his father, his dad joked about the fossils being the remains of someone's Kentucky Fried Chicken dinner tossed from a car window. The two were looking for shark's teeth in the yellow-gray, shallow marine muds of the Paw Paw Formation. They knew they were on to something, so they brought the bones to my lab. What Johnny had found turned out to be something's dinner, all right, but it was not chicken. It was a dinosaur. It was the first baby nodosaur that has ever been found, and it came from within the city limits of Fort Worth. Dinosaur fossils are not usually found in cities, simply because for whatever reason, cities are not often built upon rocks that preserve them. The finding of this dinosaur, as well as the find itself, is exciting, because the discovery was made by a kid in a city. The public television program "Reading Rainbow" portrayed a reenactment of it, which was good, except that it did not adequately display the work and enthusiasm Johnny put into the find, and it made the paleontologist look like a nerd.

Nodosaurs are armored dinosaurs related to ankylosaurs. They walked on all fours and held their heads low to the ground. Their teeth have the leaf shape of primitive herbivorous dinosaurs. The specimen that Johnny found represents the oldest species of the family to be found in Texas.

Johnny's nodosaur was a baby. Its thigh bone is only about four inches long. The ends of the limb bones are not well formed, and the arches of the backbone that protect the spinal cord had not grown together with the rest of the vertebrae, a sure sign that the dinosaur was an infant. It was newly hatched from the egg. No bony armor was found, perhaps because the plates, or scutes, from which it was made were first formed in cartilage that was replaced by bone as the animal grew. Perhaps Johnny's dinosaur was too young to have developed bone in its skin. I like to call Johnny's baby nodosaur a scuteling. That seems to be an appropriate name with a nice ring to it.

Johnny and his father worked diligently to find every scrap of the scuteling that remained in the ground. There was quite a bit of it. There were teeth and bits of the skull. Even though only a sampling of the vertebrae was found, the ones that are from all the areas of the spine: neck, back, pelvis, and tail. Parts, but not all, of the front legs and of the hind legs were found. There was a broken fragment of a shoulder blade, one complete upper-arm bone and part of the other, a piece of the pelvis, a thigh bone, parts of the lower limb, and even a squat toe claw. Bits from everywhere in the skeleton are there, but it was not 100 percent complete. That is a very strange pattern.

All of the bones from Johnny's scuteling, when examined closely, show interesting scratches and punctures. Moreover, oysters are attached to some of them. Those are big clues to a story about Johnny's dinosaur that makes sense. Just like the discovery, it is an amazing story.

A population of nodosaurs frequented the shore along the southeastern edge of the great Western Interior Seaway to lay their eggs. Soon after hatching, Johnny's scuteling ended up in the water. I do not know whether it was alive or dead when it got there. If it was alive, it soon drowned. If it was dead, it had not been fed upon by any creatures before it was immersed. We know that because Johnny and his dad found parts of all areas of the body. The scuteling had to have been whole when it sank to the bottom of the Paw Paw sea.

The waters in which the Paw Paw Formation was deposited were not brackish but were at least of normal ocean saltiness, judging from the diverse assemblage of marine animals found fossilized in the sediments. There are abundant starfish and sea urchins, clams, and other kinds of invertebrates.

Pawpawsaurus frequented the shore of the ancient sea, as this herd is doing while some young are washed away. Illustration by Karen Carr, courtesy Fort Worth Museum of Science and History.

There are crabs and small sharks. These last two are particularly important for figuring out the fossilization history of the scuteling.

After the baby nodosaur entered the water and sank to the bottom, its flesh was scavenged and ripped from its body. Sharks tore at the meat, rasping it from the bone. Crabs pulled and wrestled the carcass. If they were large enough, they could haul off a joint or a vertebra. The action of the scavengers explains why each remaining bone is scratched and punctured. It also explains why parts—but not all—of each area of the skeleton are present, from head to toe to tail. What was found is what was left behind by scavengers.

After the bones were stripped of their flesh, they lay hard and clean on the soft mud of the ocean floor, but only for a short time. Oyster spat, the tiny larvae that search for a firm spot to anchor their shells, settled on the bones and grew to a length of three-quarters of an inch. Then they died, indicating that sediments blanketed the bones, smothering the oysters.

You can ask an oyster expert how long it takes for an oyster to grow to be three-quarters of an inch long. You will be told that it depends on how much food is available and how warm the water is. Without knowing a number of variables, the answer is very inexact. However, oysters the size of those found on the scuteling could have reached their size in a month.

Now we can put the whole story—one possible story, anyway—of Johnny's nodosaur together.

One day in the long-distant past, a nodosaur scuteling hatched from its egg near the edge of the sea. It tottered from its nest and fell into the water, squeaking with terror. As its mother looked on in agony, the scuteling disappeared beneath the blue water. In no time small sharks and crabs attacked the carcass, reducing it to bare bones in a number of hours. The hard bones that remained made a perfect substrate on which oyster spat could settle, but the oysters were doomed to suffocate because of the gentle rain of silt and sand deposited from the water.

How long did all this take, the hatching, dying, scavenging, encrusting, and burial? It may have taken no more than one month. All those were the events that occurred between 97.5 and 100 million years ago during the one-month life, death, and burial of a baby dinosaur. And all of this story is a result of the discovery and responsible action of a ten-year-old kid, Johnny Maurice.

What is more, as quadrupedal, armored herbivores, nodosaurs resemble nothing so much in the modern world as they do armadillos, the quintessential animal of Texas. Johnny's scuteling is about the size of an armadillo. There is no meaningful connection, of course, between armadillos and nodosaurs, but I cannot put from my mind the vision of an armadillo-like dinosaur inhabiting the heart of Texas 100 million years before the invention of highways!

Johnny's was not the first discovery of nodosaurs in the heart of Texas, and it has not been the last. The first that I know of was made many decades ago. It was found near Blue Mound, now almost a part of Fort Worth, and was sent to the Smithsonian Institution in Washington, D.C. It is not a very good specimen, just a few scrappy bones, but it was used to named a new genus and species, *Texasetes pleurohalio* (TEX-us-EET-es plur-uh-HALE-ee-o), which means "Texas dweller who lived by the sea." Unfortunately, the question has arisen as to whether the fossils used to name *Texasetes* are adequate

Johnny's scuteling falls into the ocean. Illustration by Karen Carr.

Twelve-year-old Johnny Maurice found the nodosaur scuteling in Fort Worth while he was out with his dad. The discovery was reenacted on the public television show Reading Rainbow. *Courtesy of John C. Maurice.*

to prove that it is a new and different species. Other bones found in Tarrant County suggest that naming *Texasetes* may not have been the best thing to do because the material does not uniquely define a new dinosaur.

Other recent nodosaur finds do define a new species, however, which cannot be shown to belong to *Texasetes.* Nineteen-year-old Cameron Campbell, who works at the Fort Worth Zoo, found an absolutely beautiful skull of an adult nodosaur near where Johnny found the scuteling. There were a few parts missing, until Johnny's father and Rob Reid found more pieces of the skull. Now it is almost totally complete, missing only some teeth and a few minor bits here and there. Rob also found part of another skeleton.

The skull is undistorted. It even has a pair of bony eyelids preserved with it. This specimen clearly demonstrates that a new kind of nodosaur lived here. It is being named *Pawpawsaurus campbelli* (paw-paw-SAWR-us CAM-bul-eye), after the person who found the diagnostic skull. If you want to see *Pawpawsaurus,* you have only to go to the Fort Worth Museum of Science and History. Johnny's scuteling and Cameron's skull are on display there.

Oh, what wonderful fossils come from the Paw Paw! Another one of my favorites was found by my friend Chris Wadleigh. He brought in the front end of the snout of a strange critter. The bone of the snout is paper thin. Tooth sockets show that the first teeth stick out toward the front. The top of the snout rises up into a flange. All these features show that this is not an ordinary vertebrate fossil. It is the snout of a pterosaur, a flying reptile that soared above the Paw Paw sea, swooping down to capture fish, its light head stabilized by the keel on its nose cutting through the water.

This pterosaur is a new species, too. It is *Coloborhynchus wadleighi* (cul-ah-bu-RINK-us WAD-lee-eye), named for Chris. The genus *Coloborhynchus* was named in the last century by Sir Richard Owen, who based the name on fossils from the Hastings Sands of England. *Coloborhynchus wadleighi* is the first record of this genus in North America. It is also the first time a pterosaur with a flange at the front of the snout has been found in North America, although they are also known from South America as well as England. And it is the only pterosaur known from all of the Cretaceous Period in North America that had teeth.

The conditions for fossilization are clearly special in the Paw Paw. The formation represents a time when the sea was shallow and the water quiet, with just the right amount of sedimentation. Unfortunately, those times did not last. Sea level rose again, and for the next five million years, maybe less, the heart of Texas was well under water. No dinosaurs are known here until the waters receded once more and deltaic deposits of the Woodbine Formation began to form. The youngest dinosaurs in Texas are found in the Woodbine.

The most prolific source for dinosaurs in the Woodbine Formation is in the area of the Dallas–Fort Worth International Airport. That is also the farthest east in the state where dinosaurs are known to occur. All the other rocks ranging in age up to the end of the Cretaceous and lying to the east of DFW airport are marine in origin. None has produced a dinosaur so far as I know. No dinosaurs lived in that part of East Texas during those times because it was all under water, and no dinosaurs that might have gotten washed into the sea have been found. Even without dinosaurs, the rocks east of DFW airport have lots and lots of interesting fossils, among which are plesiosaurs and mosasaurs, two kinds of very large and exciting marine reptiles. Long-necked plesiosaurs are the reptiles after which the mythical Loch Ness monster is fashioned. So right on the airport grounds of DFW, dinosaur fossils have been found on the Fort Worth side. On the Dallas side, plesiosaurs have been found in the marine rocks. That is truly amazing. One million people a week pass through that airport and over those bones. No other airport I know has dinosaurs right on the grounds, safe under the runways—and DFW has sea monsters, too!

There are a number of depositional environments represented in the Woodbine Formation, ranging from fully marine to fully riverine. Sea level fluctuated rapidly during part of Woodbine time while river deltas built seaward and migrated laterally. Most of the bones from the Woodbine at DFW are fragmentary because they are reworked from layers in which they were originally entombed. They were eroded out by a minor transgression to be deposited as a lag at the base of the succeeding stratum. Lag deposits are composed of particles too large or heavy for the currents to winnow away. At DFW, bones and teeth of dinosaurs are found as a lag with pebbles and scraps of fossil crocodiles, turtles, frogs, bony fish, sharks, rays, and even a mammal.

There are at least four kinds of dinosaurs known from the Woodbine.

Theropod meat-eaters are identified from a few isolated teeth. Nodosaurs are known from teeth and a few bones: an upper arm, part of a leg, and some bony armor. Enough of the nodosaur is known to conclude that it is not the same genus as *Pawpawsaurus*. The third kind of dinosaur is an iguanodont, a big ornithopod plant eater, known from a few teeth. With such scrappy material it is hard to be certain about the identification. If correct, this could be the youngest iguanodont known from North America. The fourth kind of Woodbine dinosaur is a duck-billed hadrosaur. The presence of duckbills is very interesting because, at ninety-five million years old, these are among the oldest known hadrosaurs in all of North America.

Duckbills have a battery of many small teeth in their jaws. While an old tooth was being worn down, a new tooth was growing in to take its place. By the time the first tooth was completely worn and shed, it was not missed at all in the dental battery. Many discarded hadrosaur teeth have been found in the Woodbine. However, there are also a few vertebrae, the ankle end of a shinbone, part of the upper arm of a baby hadrosaur, and the hip end of a thighbone from nearby Lake Grapevine. That is slim pickin's, but because their significance was clear, we were poised for a big strike. And we got one. It came just as I was readying this chapter to go to press.

Sediments of the Woodbine at Lake Grapevine, just a few miles northwest from DFW airport, were deposited by streams, in deltas, and along the seacoast. Few bones have been found there, but footprints occur in several strata. Grapevine Dam lies near the town of Flower Mound. That is where the latest find was made. Gary Byrd made it.

Gary is a roofing contractor from Rockwall, east of Dallas. He has a degree in geology from the University of Texas. He is also a fossil enthusiast and a member of the Dallas Paleontological Society. Everywhere Gary goes he stops at road cuts to look for fossils. That is what happened while he was working at Flower Mound, but this time he made the find of a lifetime. On the day before Thanksgiving he found fragments of bone on the surface of the exposed Woodbine Formation. He took them to the Dallas Museum of Natural History. Bill Lowe, also of the Dallas Paleontological Society, visited the site with Gary on behalf of the museum. Because I had a student, Yuong-Nam Lee, studying the dinosaurs of the Woodbine Formation, Charles Finsley, the museum's curator, called SMU. Yuong-nam went down to the museum and identified the last knuckle of the toe of a hadrosaur among the fragments that had been picked up. Obviously we needed to find out if there was more of the beast in the ground. There was. Yuong-nam found a skull. This is the first really informative specimen of the Woodbine duckbill to come to light. We were poised for the find because we knew what its significance would be.

Duckbill dinosaurs are diverse and rather common toward the end of the Cretaceous Period, but that is not until 20 million years or so after the Woodbine Formation was deposited. At 95 million years old, the skull from Flower Mound is among the oldest hadrosaur specimens known from North America. Hadrosaurs probably did not originate here. Instead, their roots are in Asia, from which they dispersed to North America soon after their origin. The Flower Mound skull will allow a comparison with potential Asian forbears of the North American duckbills and tell us about the roots of the hadrosaur radiation in this continent. Specimens of such significance and that cause such an impact on dinosaur science are only rarely found. Not a bad day's work for Gary Byrd. Had he not taken the responsible path, the specimen might have been lost to science and no one would have learned its lessons.

From the footprints at Lake Grapevine, the height of the Woodbine duckbill is calculated to be nine feet at the hip. Now, if enough of the Flower Mound specimen is present, we may be able to test our estimate. There are other interesting features of the prints at Lake Grapevine. Dinosaur tracks usually fall in a line, and a rather straight line at that, showing the progression from one place to the next. One of the things I like most about the Grapevine tracks is that not all fall in trackways. One locality shows a highly irregular surface formed from dinosaurs tramping around. I do not know what they were doing. They just seem to be mulling around along the water's edge, out to where the bottom was rippled by the current, up on the shore to where little puddles formed in the imprints of their three-toed feet. As the water in the toe pools evaporated, the mud dried out and cracked. All this can be seen now, but probably not for long. The site is falling victim to the vicissitudes of nature and the battering of the lake shore as it rises and falls during the year.

If we look back on this second world of Texas dinosaurs that we have been examining, we see that there were great changes from its beginning in the Twin Mountains Formation to its end in the Woodbine Formation. Through it all, we can see that the dinosaurs are not the same in the beginning of this interval as they are at the end of it. There are probably several reasons for these changes, including the evolution of new species, extinction of others, changing environments and the ecological requirements of different dinosaur species, and the dispersal of new species into the area from somewhere else. There was plenty of time for all three of these possibilities to occur during the more than twenty million years that we have been discussing, but unfortunately, the fossil record is not yet complete enough for us to work out all the details of faunal change that occurred through the second world of Texas dinosaurs.

An example of the evolution of a new species might be the case of

The duckbill hadrosaur fossils found around the Dallas–Fort Worth International Airport are among the oldest in North America. This hadrosaur is shown at its nest, although no hadrosaur eggs or nests have actually been found in Central Texas—yet. Illustration by Karen Carr, courtesy Fort Worth Museum of Science and History.

Tenontosaurus. As we have seen, *Tenontosaurus dossi* occurs in the Twin Mountains Formation more than 113 million years ago. By the time of the Paluxy Formation, no younger than 105 million years ago, the genus is represented by a closely related but more advanced species of *Tenontosaurus.* Even though we can see that the species of *Tenontosaurus* are different from the Twin Mountains Formation to the Paluxy, on the whole, the dinosaur fauna of Central Texas was fairly uniform during this interval. What is surprising, perhaps even astounding, is that all of the dinosaurs known from the Twin Moun-

Gary Byrd, who discovered the 95 million-year-old site at Flower Mound, which produced one of the oldest hadrosaur skulls ever found. Photograph by Yuong-Nam Lee.

tains, Glen Rose, and Paluxy formations became extinct near the end of the Paluxy time, not less than 105 million years ago. They are gone not just in Texas but from everywhere they are known, which is primarily western North America. The extinctions included *Tenontosaurus, Pleurocoelus, Acrocanthosaurus,* the new hypsilophodont species, and, so far as we know, all of the lesser-known species. None of these animals shows up again anywhere else. As a matter of fact, there are no brontosaurs in all of North America from the time of *Pleurocoelus* until the very end of the Cretaceous, but that is a story to be told in the next chapter. The cause (or causes) of these extinctions in the middle of the Cretaceous is unknown and rarely discussed. However, the phenomenon does seem to coincide generally with the expansion of the Western Interior Seaway.

The next time dinosaurs show up in Texas, they are represented by *Pawpawsaurus,* which, being a nodosaur, represents a group of dinosaurs not known in Texas earlier than 100 million years ago. They are known from other places in North America before that time, so we can speculate that the family moved into Texas from up north. The Woodbine nodosaur is too poorly represented by fossils to conclude whether it is more closely related to the older *Pawpawsaurus* or to more northern species. The presence of duck-billed hadrosaurs in the Woodbine is particularly interesting because it is likely that they are of Asian origin. The Texas record is one of the earliest—if not the earliest—on this continent.

Of course, dinosaurs in the heart of Texas did not live alone. The communities of which they were a part were complex and viable, and they, too, were changing through time. Compared to the first world of Texas dinosaurs during the Triassic, the animals and plants of the Cretaceous are much more familiar. However, the changes in the plants between the Twin Mountains Formation and the Woodbine are profound. During the time of the Twin Mountains, Glen Rose, and Paluxy formations, the most conspicuous plants were gymnosperms related to pines, cypress, and other conifers. Flowering plants were present, as we know from pollen and leaves preserved as fossils. But it was early in the evolution of flowering plants, or angiosperms, and they were diminutive and rare. The gymnosperm trees grew to a good size, up to a couple of feet in trunk diameter. Fossil wood is often found with dinosaur bones. Cones and logs occur right next to *Pleurocoelus* at Jones Ranch. Silicified wood is common in the Paluxy Formation, even to the point of being useful as an ornamental building stone. Many old houses in Central Texas along the outcrop of Paluxy rocks have petrified conifer wood in their walls. The original Wolfe Nursery building in Stephenville was built of fossil logs.

By Woodbine time, the forests and woods of Central Texas had a completely different look from what they had in the Twin Mountains and Paluxy. Conifers were waning, and the landscape was taken over by flowering plants. Familiar trees such as sycamore relatives were prevalent. Could the change in vegetation have played a part in the change of dinosaur species during this time interval in Central Texas? Certainly it could, especially with the herbivores. But we do not yet know what caused the change in the flora, although it could have been influenced by changes in climate brought about by the mere presence of the Western Interior Seaway. Nor do we yet know the precise interrelationships between the dinosaurs and the plants of their world. We also do not know how the changes of the middle Cretaceous affected the insects and other invertebrates that were so important in the food chain. The only fossil insect we have in this part of Texas is a dragonfly wing from the Woodbine, found when fossil leaves were being excavated.

The entire animal community of Central Texas changed along with the plants and the dinosaurs. As a result of the diversity of depositional environments sampling different ecological communities, there is a great diversity of nondinosaurian animal life known. Sharks, rays, and bony fishes of various sorts thrived in freshwater streams, brackish estuaries, and lagoons. The last known North American lungfish are found in the Woodbine Formation. Frogs croaked and salamanders slithered in moist, fresh environments. Lizards were decidedly modern compared to the lizardlike animals of the Texas Triassic. Turtles and crocodiles inhabited both the land and sea, including some very nice sea turtle fossils from the Glen Rose Formation.

Pterosaurs soared among the clouds. Besides the *Coloborhynchus* pterosaur snout from the Paw Paw Formation, there is also a report of these reptiles from the Antlers Formation and from the Glen Rose. Pterosaur bones are hollow and light with thin walls, facilitating flight. As a consequence of their light structure, pterosaur bones are fragile. If they are preserved at all, they are usually crushed. The pterosaur from the Glen Rose Formation is known from a completely uncrushed and undistorted upper-arm bone. This is remarkable, but even more so because the bone was blasted out of the limestone that encased it during the construction of a cooling pond for Comanche Peak Nuclear Power Plant. The dynamite that was used to blow the rock away also freed a pterosaur fossil in perfect condition!

Mammals underwent important evolutionary changes between 105 and 95 million years ago. Most importantly for the modern world, by 95 million years ago marsupial mammals related to opossums were present, as shown by a fossil tooth from the Woodbine Formation at DFW airport. In the Twin Mountains, Glen Rose, Paluxy, and Antlers formations there are no true marsupials. Nor are there placentals, the other major group of living, live-bearing mammals, even though those formations are famous for producing mammal fossils from the middle part of the Cretaceous Period. Marsupial and placental mammals can be identified on the basis of the shape and the number of their molars. Those mammals known from the earlier part of the Texas Cretaceous section have features on their teeth that are intermediate between marsupials and placentals. They can be pigeon-holed into neither

One of the earliest known opossums is represented by one tooth from the Dallas–Fort Worth International Airport. Illustration by Karen Carr.

group but are equally related to both. They are distinct, extinct side branches on the evolutionary tree that gave rise to both marsupials and placentals. Their importance is that they show a diverse evolutionary experimentation in the Texas middle Cretaceous that culminated in the exclusive survival of placentals and marsupials to inhabit the modern world. Since we are placental mammals, this chapter in our evolutionary history has to be important because it is from these furry worm grubbers and insect eaters that later placentals—including all primates and eventually humans—emerged. The Woodbine marsupial tooth tells us that the sorting out of this evolutionary radiation into marsupials and placentals had occurred by 95 million years ago. The Antlers and Paluxy mammals tell us that it probably occurred after 105 million.

After the deltas of the Woodbine Formation had distributed their silt along the ocean front, the sea rose to cover dry land in Central Texas for the last time in the Mesozoic Era. No more would dinosaurs have a place to tread. The waters over eastern Texas teemed with all sorts of invertebrates and fish. They also became the domain of thirty-foot-long mosasaurs (overgrown seagoing lizards) and plesiosaurs of several species, including those

Ichthyornis, *a ternlike bird with teeth, soared over the ancient seas of eastern Texas. Illustration by Karen Carr.*

with long necks and those with short ones. Flying overhead and floating on the surface of the sea were ternlike birds with teeth in their jaws. The birds are called *Ichthyornis* (ick-THEE-orn-is), or "fish-bird."

While most of Texas was underwater for the remainder of the Cretaceous Period, some of the Trans-Pecos region was not. There, high and dry at the end of the Age of Reptiles, dinosaurs were free to roam. That is where we go next.

CHAPTER 4

The Land of Texas Giants

ALONG THE SOUTHWESTERN BORDER of the United States, between Texas and Mexico, the Rio Grande flows swiftly through a rugged, parched countryside dotted with cactus and baked by the sun. The river flows south, then curves its way north. Its path is known as the Big Bend of the Rio Grande. The two largest counties in Texas, Brewster and Presidio, with a combined area half the size of all New England, lie within the Big Bend. Thirteen thousand people live there. Not many. It is a land of ranches, rattlesnakes, and record high temperatures; of abandoned mercury mines, ghost towns, and chili cook-offs. It is what remains of the Wild West. And it is beautiful. It is a geological wonder. For us it is important. It was the home of the youngest dinosaurs in the state, the third world of Texas dinosaurs. The story of Big Bend dinosaurs was pieced together by Wann Langston, Jr., and his students at the University of Texas, most notably Tom Lehman, now a professor at Texas Tech University. Besides naming a new dinosaur and determining many interesting facets of Big Bend paleontology and paleoecology, Tom has put the facts together in a comprehensive way, explaining how Big Bend fits into the larger picture of dinosaur history.

The landscape of the Big Bend country does not look much like north-central Texas today, but in times long past the Glen Rose sea stretched for endless miles over the shallow platform that was to become the southern half of Texas. It stretched all the way from Glen Rose to Big Bend. Dinosaurs walked the tidal flats of much of the northeastern shore of that sea. In the southwest the waters continued on, seemingly forever. They extended over

Chasmosaurus maris-
calensis *feed on scouring
rushes and romping in the
swampy Aguja landscape
of Big Bend.* Deino-
suchus, *a giant Texas
crocodile, looks on. Illustration by Karen Carr.*

the area of the Big Bend toward the mountains that ultimately became the
Sierra Madre Occidental in Mexico. As the sea reached the region that is now
the border between the United States and Mexico, the platform dropped off
and the waters deepened rapidly. Superimposed where the platform bottom
of the shallow sea dove into the deeper ocean trough is the region now known
as Big Bend.

Rocks of the Glen Rose Formation and its equivalents were deposited all
the way from East Texas to the Rio Grande. It was all underwater. The Big
Bend remained inundated, while the terrestrial Paluxy Formation containing
the bones of dinosaurs was being deposited in north-central Texas. As time
passed in its march to the end of the Cretaceous Period, the western shore of
the ocean advanced from near the Sierra Madre Occidental toward Big Bend.
Eventually the ocean trough bordering the platform of the shallow sea was

filled with sediments, the waters withdrew, and Big Bend emerged from the depths. There, in the Aguja Formation—a rock unit deposited in the deltas, marshes, streams, and lagoons of eighty million years ago—is the record of dinosaurs wandering back to Texas. They came in from the north. They had been gone from the state since the time of the Woodbine Formation because for the intervening fifteen million years, there was a dearth of dry land and a prevalence of ocean.

While the Big Bend emerged on its way to becoming completely high and dry, most of Texas remained submerged under the sea until well into the Age of Mammals. The Panhandle was out of the water at the end of the Cretaceous, but eastern and southern Texas were not. When dinosaurs began to forage at Big Bend, *Ichthyornis,* like a gull, flew the skies and floated atop the ocean waters above what is now Kansas and Central Texas, where they have been found as fossils. At that stage, while Big Bend was an area of coastal swamps and deltas and the rest of Texas was underwater, the continent of North America was divided in half by the Western Interior Seaway, separating the land into two masses. The western land mass was like a huge finger of land, a peninsula, projecting southward from the eastern extremity of Asia. The interior seaway isolated it from the east. Big Bend was the southern part of the western land mass.

During the final stage of the Cretaceous Period, the Western Interior Seaway withdrew from the land. It pulled back north toward the Arctic Ocean and south toward the ancient Gulf of Mexico. The eastern and western flanks of the seaway joined, connecting the land of each half of the continent once more. The connection grew larger as the seaway fled to the north and south.

The Aguja Formation is the oldest of the two major dinosaur-bearing rock units in Big Bend. The second formation is called the Javelina, which overlies and is therefore younger than the Aguja. The Aguja sediments represent environmental conditions when the sea first receded and exposed land in the Big Bend area. At that time, between eighty-four million and seventy-four million years ago, the Western Interior Seaway was complete. The Aguja was being deposited in the southern part of the western American peninsular land mass, on the western shore of the seaway.

However, the configuration of the shoreline at Big Bend continued to change. It moved eastwardly with time until, at the end of the Cretaceous Period, it lay some 240 miles to the east of where it had started. The end of the Cretaceous was also an important time for mountain building in western North America. Great blocks of the Earth were uplifted along faults to form highlands. Rivers meandered through the adjacent valleys, occasionally overflowing their banks to spread silt across the floodplain, burying the rich soils that developed there. That is the geological setting of Big Bend during the last stage of the Cretaceous. The rock unit resulting from the deposition of river sands and muds in channels and on the floodplains is called the Javelina Formation. It ranges from about seventy-four million years in age to the end of the Mesozoic at sixty-six million.

The Javelina Formation is a sequence of purple, red, gray, and green mudstone layers. The mudstones contain abundant limy nodules. Interbedded with the mudstones are lenses of sand. The sand lenses are the remnants of ancient stream channels, and the colorful bands of mudstone represent overbank floodplain deposits on which soils were repeatedly developed. The nodules are the products of soil formation. The environment was warm but not strongly seasonal. There are suggestions of long-term climatic trends when periods of aridity, perhaps thousands of years long, alternated with extended periods of more humid conditions.

Both angiosperm and gymnosperm plants were present in the Aguja and the Javelina. Six kinds of trees are known from the Aguja; however, a new kind of tree, *Javelinoxylon* (HAVE-a-leen-OX-uh-lon), based on fossil wood, has been named for the formation in which it was found. One trunk is over two feet in diameter, indicating that trees at least ninety feet tall grew on the Javelina landscape. *Javelinoxylon* does not show well-defined growth rings, consistent with the interpretation of the lack of strong seasonality in the Cretaceous at Big Bend. Termites seem to have liked *Javelinoxylon*. Their tunnels and galleries invaded the wood soon after the plant died. Frass—termite fecal pellets—fill some of the galleries eaten out by these insects, indicating that the tree had not decayed before it was colonized. These were dry-wood termites.

As we have seen, the Aguja and Javelina formations were formed under different environmental conditions and in different geological settings. It should not be surprising that the dinosaurs and other fossil vertebrates found in the two formations often represent different species as well. A distinct and separate animal community inhabited the environment in which the Aguja Formation was deposited, and that community was replaced by the fauna of the Javelina.

Nevertheless, the dinosaurs in both of these formations are in some ways more familiar to us than the older dinosaurs of the first two worlds of Texas dinosaurs. They include horned dinosaurs, advanced duck-billed hadrosaurs, and the ever-popular *T. rex,* in addition to several other species. There are bones of both baby and adult dinosaurs known from Big Bend. There are even eggshell fragments.

It is important to keep in mind that the dinosaurs of Big Bend inhabited a land that was not out of the sea until most of the rest of Texas was underwater, and had been for at least fifteen million years. Thus, the creatures whose remains are found at Big Bend have at best a complex and circuitous relationship with older Texas dinosaurs. Some, like the horned dinosaurs, are not closely related at all, tracing their ancestry back to other continents during the time Big Bend was underwater and dinosaurs stalked north-central Texas instead.

The oldest of the dinosaur-bearing formations in the Big Bend, the Aguja, was deposited as the ocean withdrew. There are lots of fossils in the Aguja, but unfortunately they are not very complete. Dinosaur bones are most often found alone and isolated from other bones. Sometimes a bunch of scattered bones are found in the same area in a bone bed. Depending on the spot, the bones might belong to a few individuals of a number of different species; or, at other localities, there might be a lot of individuals of only a few species. Either way, complete skeletons are never found. Partial skeletons and scattered bones lying together in the same bone bed usually are arranged as if they came to rest in a depression, like a long-gone shallow pool of water. If any bones of a partial skeleton are found together and articulated as in life, the bones remaining assembled are likely to be a part of the spinal column. Vertebrae of the backbone seem to stay together longer than the rest of the skeleton, at least in the Aguja. Some bones were broken and slightly degraded by weather before they were buried and fossilized. Others seem to have been broken after burial by compression of the sediments. They do not seem to be lined up or arranged in any special way, although they are often found in clay underlying sandy channel deposits. Some of the bones are at odd angles to the horizontal, as if they had been pushed down in the original mud. Thus, the occurrence of bones in the Aguja Formation is very different from what we have seen in the first world of Texas dinosaurs at the Post Quarry or in the second world at Proctor Lake. How can the occurrence of dinosaur bones in the Aguja be explained?

The Aguja Formation is drab in color, with black, coaly layers that were built from the remains of plants accumulating in swamps near the coast. Sandier layers were deposited by rivers and streams as they built deltas into the sea. Between the stream and river channels, the land remained low and marshy. Water-loving plants blanketed the lowlands, providing a rich source of fodder for plant-eating dinosaurs. The lowlands were frequented by horned ceratopsians and duck-billed hadrosaurs, by less-common armored ankylosaurs and theropods, and by several other kinds of dinosaurs.

Occasionally one of the dinosaurs would die. Sometimes several of the same species would die at once in a mass catastrophe—perhaps around a dwindling water supply during a drought, perhaps when a norther blew through. Their bodies fell to the mud and rotted in the dark, swampy waters. Every now and then scavengers would tear at the putrid flesh, but the scavengers do not seem to have been very common. The carcasses began to dismember, starting first at the toes and extremities as they lay half-submerged. The spinal column was the last part of the skeleton to fall apart.

As the dead lay decomposed and scattered, herbivores wandered the area while they fed, trampling the bones of those that died before into the mud, occasionally squishing one end of a bone down as it was stepped on so it no longer lay in a horizontal position. Some bones were crushed and broken from the trampling. Those that survived total destruction were sealed from further degradation by flooding events, which broke through stream channels, spreading a blanketing layer of protective sand over the surface.

The most common dinosaur in the Aguja is a horned dinosaur, *Chasmosaurus mariscalensis* (KAZ-moh-SAWR-us mar-is-CAL-ins-is), named by Tom Lehman for bones collected in the Big Bend. The number of bones of this animal recovered is fairly large, and they have been found throughout the Aguja. Remains of ten to fifteen individuals were recovered from just one single bone bed. Juveniles, subadult, and fully adult animals are represented. Unfortunately, the bones are mostly isolated and disarticulated.

Horned dinosaurs of the family Ceratopsidae have a good fossil record in North America (particularly in Alberta, Montana, and Wyoming), and they have close, yet more primitive, relatives in Asia. None of the ceratopsids is older than the Late Cretaceous, and late in the Late Cretaceous at that. The most conspicuous characteristic of the horned dinosaur family is, of course, their horns. The usual configuration is to have brow horns above the eyes, another toward the end of the nose, and a smallish one on the cheek. The relative sizes and shapes of these horns are variable.

Ceratopsids are also characterized by having long heads, much of which is a broad frill of bone that extends over the neck and shoulder region. The frill varies in size, structure, and ornamentation from species to species. The margin may be beautified with additional horns, as in *Styracosaurus* (sty-RACK-uh-SAWR-us), or more simply scalloped by the presence of extra bones along the edge. In some horned dinosaurs the frill is long, with large holes or windows perforating it. In others, the frill is shorter and lacks windows.

All horned dinosaurs have a narrow beak or rostrum that lacks teeth. Behind the rostrum, batteries of teeth line the jaws. Going backward from the narrow rostrum, the skull flares to become wider in the cheek region, giving the head from top view a triangular appearance. The head was held low, and because horned dinosaurs walked on all fours, it is reasonable to assume that they fed on herbaceous and low-growing vegetation.

After Lehman described the species *Chasmosaurus mariscalensis* from Big Bend based on an extensive but fragmentary suite of fossils, a nearly complete skull of it was found. It showed that the frill in an adult could have as many as ten scallops along the edge. Younger individuals had fewer. This species clearly varies in a number of skeletal features. With all this variation in just one species, multiplied by the presence of a dozen or so other genera in North America, it seems amazing that the horned dinosaur family can be divided simply into two groups based on the frills. But it can. *Chasmosaurus* belongs in the same group as *Triceratops*.

Lehman was able to piece together a great deal of information about his new species, even though the specimens with which he had to work were disarticulated. *Chasmosaurus mariscalensis* had a short, stocky nose horn. The brow horns varied in size with the individual, ranging from roughenings above the eyes in the young to large, solid, upwardly curved structures in older members of the species. Even in the adults the brow horns varied: some individuals having more curved and flaring horns; others with more erect and parallel horns.

There are two reasons why the horns in *Chasmosaurus mariscalensis* are so variable from individual to individual. The first is because the horns grew as the animal grew, so they vary with age. The second reason is a sexual hypothesis. The horns may have been different in males and females. The horns were more curved and divergent from each other, perhaps, in the females. In the presumed males, the horns were more massive, erect and parallel, facing directly out from the skull in front of the face, making them more formidable weapons.

It is not at all surprising to think of horns as exhibiting differences between males and females. They do so now in most species of mammals that possess them. Moreover, horns are functional. They are very important in the behavior of a species, in the way individuals interact with one another: in competing for mates or territory, for instance. In fact, in many cases, horns and the behavior that involves their use are likely to be more important for competition, territorial disputes, and establishing the pecking order within the species than for behaviors that involve other species, such as in defense. In the ceratopsids, the horns and frill are most often assumed to have been primarily for defense: the horns ready to impale, and the frill shielding the neck. That may have been true, but those structures may have served other functions as well. It is equally likely that horns and frills in ceratopsids were important features in the social organization of the species.

The occurrence of *Chasmosaurus* in bone beds at Big Bend has some interesting implications. Recall that Lehman's sample had juvenile, subadult, and adult individuals, all found together. Why were those individuals found together as they were?

Perhaps the answer lies in the way they lived. Horned dinosaurs of several different species have been found at various places in the North American West in bone beds and mass concentrations. They were most likely victims of floods, fire, or some other disaster that killed a large proportion of an assembled group or herd. Perhaps most or all species of horned dinosaurs lived in herds that roamed over the landscape. As the combined feeding activities of a large number of individuals dining together depleted resources in one area they moved on to the next, thus allowing the vegetation in the grazed area to recover and provide them fodder another time. In the case of *Chasmosaurus mariscalensis,* the fact that a range of individual ages—young, subadult, and adult—was found in a single quarry at Big Bend implies that some sort of catastrophic event caused the death of a herd or some part of it. Perhaps it was a drought that brought death in a short period of time to a lot of individuals. Perhaps it was a freeze. Maybe a group became mired. Regardless of the cause, after a severe blow to the herd, the low-lying environmental conditions of the Aguja provided for the victims' becoming entombed and preserved.

The horned dinosaur Torosaurus *carefully eyes the scene as* Tyrannosaurus *feeds on* Alamosaurus. *Illustration by Karen Carr.*

Chasmosaurus mariscalensis may be the best-known dinosaur from the Big Bend, but it is known only from the Aguja Formation, not the overlying Javelina. The ceratopsid from the Javelina Formation is different. It is called *Torosaurus utahensis* (TOR-uh-SAWR-us YOU-tah-ins-is). It, too, belongs in the same group of ceratopsids as *Triceratops* and *Chasmosaurus.* The most obvious difference between the Big Bend horned dinosaurs is that the brow horns of *Torosaurus* curve downward and forward toward the nose rather than backward and upward as in *Chasmosaurus.* There are suggestions of other kinds of horned dinosaurs in the Javelina in addition to *Torosaurus,* but the remains are so scrappy that it is hard to say with any confidence to which species they belong. More work needs to be done.

Aside from being the best-known dinosaur from Big Bend, *Chasmosaurus mariscalensis* is also one of the most common in the Aguja. The other common Aguja dinosaur is *Kritosaurus navajovius* (KRITE-uh-SAWR-us NAH-vuh-HOH-vee-us), a duck-billed hadrosaur. (Some authorities do not accept the name *Kritosaurus* and include it with *Gryposaurus* [GRIPE-uh-SAWR-us]. That need not concern us here.) Its head was wide and flat, with the bones near the front of the skull humping up to form a distinct "Roman nose." *Kritosaurus,*

like *Chasmosaurus,* is known from the Aguja but not the Javelina Formation. Other hadrosaurs are known from the Javelina, but here, too, the material is so scrappy that the identifications are tenuous. Something like *Edmontosaurus* (ed-MONT-uh-SAWR-us), a forty-foot-long hadrosaur, might have been the big duckbill of the Javelina.

The largest of Big Bend's dinosaurs is *Alamosaurus,* from the Javelina Formation only. It is a sauropodomorph, as is *Pleurocoelus* from the older rocks of the second world of Texas dinosaurs. However, *Alamosaurus* is of a different family, the titanosaurids, that is not known in North America prior to their occurrence at Big Bend.

Alamosaurus is a good Texas-sounding name, but its name is a bit misleading. It was not named for the Alamo, in San Antonio. Its name comes from something else. The cottonwood tree—*alamo,* in Spanish—has deep roots and draws water from far under the ground. A cottonwood grew near a spring at an old Navajo trading post in New Mexico, the Ojo Alamo. The name of the dinosaur came from the trading post because it was in those same badlands where *Alamosaurus* bones were first found early in this century. Since then they have turned up in Utah, Wyoming, and the Big Bend of Texas.

Alamosaurus was Big Bend's largest giant, but it was a plant eater and not necessarily vicious. The title of Big Bend's fiercest dinosaur goes to the most popular dinosaur of all time. *Tyrannosaurus rex* lived in Big Bend. At least it seems to be *T. rex.* The identification is based on a piece of an upper jaw with large, slicing teeth from the Javelina Formation. The jaw is shaped just differently enough from other *T. rex* jaws to raise the possibility that it could be a new, unnamed giant. Until that can be proven, however, I go along with its being *T. rex,* the top carnivore at the end of the Mesozoic Era.

A few more of Big Bend's lesser-known dinosaurs should be mentioned. Among plant eaters, fragments of a hypsilophodont have been found in the Aguja. *Stegoceras* (steg-OHS-uh-rus), a hundred-pound, dome-skulled pachycephalosaur, may be present in the same formation. Armored dinosaurs, known mainly from the bony plates that formed in their skin, have been found in both the Aguja and the Javelina. There are two families of armored dinosaurs. The first family, the nodosaurids, is represented by *Panoplosaurus* (PAN-op-luh-SAWR-us) in the Aguja and by an unidentified representative in the Javelina. The other family of armored dinosaurs, the ankylosaurids, is represented by mini-van–sized *Euoplocephalus* (YOO-op-luh-SEF-uh-lus) in the Aguja, and a few fragments in the Javelina that are only identifiable as ankylosaurid.

The meat eaters among Big Bend's list of lesser-known dinosaur celebrities include something like *Albertosaurus* (al-BURT-uh-SAWr-us) or

Daspletosaurus (das-PLEET-uh-SAWR-us) from both the Aguja and Javelina formations. Smaller, enigmatic remains have been referred to *Paronychodon* (PAR-uh-NIKE-uh-don) in the Aguja and *Troodon* (TROH-uh-don) in both. An unidentified ostrich mimic is known from the Aguja.

If all this is boiled down—what we know well and what requires more study—we see that there are clearly differences between the fossil fauna found in the Aguja Formation and that from the Javelina. The Aguja fauna could be characterized most obviously as having *Chasmosaurus* and *Kritosaurus,* while the Javelina has a different horned dinosaur, *Torosaurus,* plus it has *T. rex* and *Alamosaurus.* The differences in the faunas reflect the amount of time that separates the two and, at least to some degree, the environmental changes that occurred as the coastal habitat of the Aguja was replaced by the inland floodplain environment of the Javelina. The kinds of dinosaurs reflect their habitat, their environment, and their evolutionary histories.

The restriction of dinosaur species to specific habitats can be seen all across western North America during the Late Cretaceous. *Javelinoxylon* and other fossil plants seem to suggest a similar pattern. Part of that phenomenon may be related to the large latitudinal gradient between northern and southern localities, with different species adapting to the climatic regimes of different areas. That seems to be the case with *Chasmosaurus mariscalensis* from the Aguja. Different species of *Chasmosaurus* are known from more northerly localities of Wyoming, Montana, South Dakota, and Alberta, Canada. However, the situation is more complicated in the Javelina Formation.

The Javelina has species that are known far and wide in western North America. Most notable among these are *Tyrannosaurus rex* and *Torosaurus utahensis.* Nevertheless, other elements of the fauna exhibit a remarkable zoogeographic pattern. The sauropod *Alamosaurus,* for instance, is not known from the higher-latitude localities of western North America north of southern Wyoming. The pattern we see is probably realistic because some of the best localities of the Late Cretaceous are in Montana, Alberta, and Saskatchewan, and there is a decent record of dinosaurs from the North Slope of Alaska as well. Dinosaurs show definite geographic patterns.

Lehman examined the distribution of all the dinosaurs in North America during the last stage of the Cretaceous Period. He concluded that three distinct assemblages can be recognized, each restricted to a specific environment. The three assemblages are named after their predominant herbivorous member. One is named for the ceratopsid *Triceratops.* The second derives its name from *Leptoceratops* (LEPT-uh-SER-uh-tops), which is a protoceratopsid. This family is closely related to the ceratopsid horned dinosaurs but is more primitive and lacks well-developed horns. The third assemblage is the

Alamosaurus fauna. The dinosaurs comprising the assemblages are not completely mutually exclusive among these three groups. *Tyrannosaurus rex,* for example, occurs in all three, while *Torosaurus* is found in both the *Triceratops* and *Alamosaurus* faunas.

The distribution of these three faunal assemblages is influenced by the north-south latitudinal gradient and by local environmental factors. You will recall that the end of the Cretaceous was characterized by mountain building and the retreat of the Western Interior Seaway. The Pacific shoreline was also retreating to the west during the same interval. The provincialism of the three faunas during this time of environmental instability attests to the evolutionary adaptability of dinosaurs in general. Species characteristic of each environmentally discrete region evolved and dispersed in response to the physical parameters governing their lives. Therefore, different regions exhibit different suites of species.

The *Triceratops* fauna inhabited the western side of the Western Interior Seaway in humid, swampy coastal lowlands; flat alluvial plains along river courses; and the gentle rises leading to more mountainous countryside. It occurs from Saskatchewan to northern Colorado. The heart of the assemblage seems to be focused around the shrinking northern lobe of the interior sea. More so than the other two assemblages, this one is dominated by a single herbivore, *Triceratops.* It is the most common dinosaur fossil. Also included in this group is the hadrosaur *Edmontosaurus,* which appears to be more common in the southern part of the range of the *Triceratops* assemblage. This hadrosaur possibly occurs in the *Alamosaurus* fauna of Big Bend in the Javelina Formation. Minor members include small and large theropods, pachycephalosaurs, ankylosaurs, *Torosaurus,* and hypsilophodonts.

The *Leptoceratops* fauna occurs from Alberta south to Wyoming. It is less well defined than the other two assemblages and seems to grade into the *Triceratops* fauna. Its definition relies mainly on the observation that where *Leptoceratops* is common, *Triceratops* is not. Conversely, where *Triceratops* is common, *Leptoceratops* is rare. The *Leptoceratops* fauna inhabited the cool environments and foothills flanking mountainous regions west of the retreating northern lobe of the interior sea. Other dinosaurs in the assemblage are similar to those of the *Triceratops* fauna.

The *Alamosaurus* fauna is more southerly in distribution. It geographically overlaps the more northerly *Triceratops* and *Leptoceratops* faunas in southern Wyoming and northern Colorado at around thirty-five degrees north latitude. The *Alamosaurus* fauna inhabited river basins between mountains where the climate was warm and rather dry. It is known from southern Wyoming, central Utah, New Mexico, and Texas, most notably at Big Bend. Occurring with *Alamosaurus* are small ceratopsids, *Torosaurus, T. rex* and other rare meat eaters, and *hadrosaurs.*

The occurrence of *Alamosaurus* in the southern part of western North America is particularly interesting because of the absence of sauropods in North America for the 40 million years prior to their occurrence at Big Bend. The sauropod giants like *Apatosaurus, Diplodocus,* and *Brachiosaurus* (BRACK-ee-uh-SAWR-us) inhabited the Earth around 150 million years ago or so. That was the sauropod heyday, more or less in the middle of the Age of Dinosaurs. Then those familiar giants died out. After their heyday, sauropods became scarce in North America. During the second world of Texas dinosaurs, at Glen Rose and other places, the footprints and bones of *Pleurocoelus* are found in rocks as young as 105 million years old. Then it, too, vanishes like the sauropods before it. All of the sauropods disappear from North America for some 35 to 40 million years. Then, as abruptly as they disappeared, sauropods are back. Just before the great extinction event that wiped out dinosaurs so efficiently at the end of the Cretaceous, *Alamosaurus* shows up on the North American scene. Because *Alamosaurus,* while obviously a sauropod, is not known from rocks older than the last stage of the Late Cretaceous in North America and because it is of a different sauropod family from all those known previously on this continent, it begs the question of its origin. Where were the sauropods for all those millions of years when they were not in North America? Where did *Alamosaurus* come from?

The answer to that first question—where were the North American sauropods after 105 and before 70 million years ago—seems easy to answer. They died out without issue on this continent. They lived on elsewhere in the world, but not here. Because they existed elsewhere, a representative of the group—but not a former North American inhabitant—later dispersed back to this continent. That is why sauropods reappear in North America toward the end of the Cretaceous. After their reappearance they lived here in the form of *Alamosaurus* right up until the great extinction at the end of the Cretaceous. At that time *T. rex, Triceratops,* and all the other dinosaur favorites alive during the final stage of the Cretaceous went extinct. *Alamosaurus* was the very last of the very large dinosaurs ever to have existed—not just in Texas, but in all probability anywhere in the world.

Alamosaurus belongs to a distinct family, the titanosaurids. The Late Cretaceous North American sauropod is not particularly closely related to the sauropods that lived in North America 105 million years ago, and it has no known probable ancestors on this continent. That brings us to the second question: where did *Alamosaurus* come from?

Alamosaurus is a migrant from the south and belongs to the titanosaurid family. This was a very widespread group of dinosaurs that was scattered across the Mesozoic globe, although no other North American sauropods belong to the family. It is most abundant in South America but is also known from Africa and Madagascar, Europe, India, and, of course, from North America, where its sole member is *Alamosaurus*. Although its roots may be traced back to the Late Jurassic, when most families of sauropods—there are a half-dozen or so—differentiated, the titanosaurid family is most characteristic of the Cretaceous Period. During the Cretaceous, all other families except titanosaurids decline. They blossom. As a matter of fact, titanosaurids are the most common family of sauropods known from the Cretaceous.

Despite their abundance and widespread distribution, until recently the titanosaurids have been relatively neglected and forgotten in dinosaur paleontology. Some paleontologists, mainly from the northern hemisphere, instead of examining titanosaurids critically, took them to be a wastebasket for the sauropods of the southern hemisphere and their significance was unrecognized. This is a status the family surely never deserved. That changed with a resurgence of paleontology in South America, which included new fieldwork and the study of more sauropod fossils. The results that were obtained tended to focus the spotlight on the real value of titanosaurids as fossils with an important biogeographic story to tell. In addition to the important work done by South American paleontologists, my colleagues and I have spent a decade doing fieldwork in the southeast African country of Malawi. We have been excavating titanosaurid bones and studying their remains in order to find out more about the origin of the family and to trace its evolutionary history.

Titanosaurid fossils are fairly widespread across the globe. They are common in South America all through the latter part of the Age of Dinosaurs, and that is the most likely place from which to derive *Alamosaurus*. But that raises two more questions: when was the Isthmus of Panama elevated from the oceans to form a land bridge between North and South America, and where did the South American titanosaurids come from? To answer these questions we must once again examine ancient geography. It allows much of what we have seen so far to be summarized.

The earliest known record of titanosaurids is usually considered to lie in rocks of about 150 million years ago in Africa. At that time, Africa and South America were conjoined. The southern part of the Atlantic Ocean did not connect with the more northern part until 100 million years ago or so. Thus, titanosaurids could roam across the joined continents of South America and Africa until the Atlantic formed a watery barrier between the two. At the time Africa was connected to South America, North America was not. The sea extended all the way up to where Dallas and Fort Worth are now. The dinosaurs in Texas, then, as discussed in chapter 3, were very unlike those living at the same time in South America or Africa.

After South America and Africa drifted apart, the titanosaurids of South America evolved on a continent that was for all essential purposes isolated for at least thirty million years. Then South America and North America became tenuously joined through Central America. All that time, while the southern Atlantic was becoming wider and titanosaurids were thriving in South America, North America was undergoing geographic changes of its own. We have seen that the ancestral Gulf of Mexico continued to grow northward, inundating what is now the Dallas–Fort Worth metroplex. It continued on beyond until western North America was cut off from the east by the Western Interior Seaway, which ran between the gulf and the Arctic Ocean. While eastern Texas still lay underwater, what is now Big Bend emerged at the western edge of the sea, a part of the peninsula extending from eastern Asia. As the Aguja Formation was deposited, the horned dinosaurs, immigrants from Asia, began to filter down and dwell along the shore. Only after that time did the link between South America and western North America form, allowing the titanosaurids to disperse northward. That is when *Alamosaurus* established itself in Big Bend.

How did *Alamosaurus* get to Big Bend? It walked along an inter-American free trade zone established late in the Age of Dinosaurs. The dispersal zone worked in both directions. In addition to *Alamosaurus* coming north, some dinosaurs headed south—especially hadrosaurs, hypsilophodonts, and possibly even horned dinosaurs.

Titanosaurid sauropods as a group have some interesting features. For one thing, some of them have bony armor in their skin. It is the only sauropod family known to have that feature, but apparently not all species of the family exhibit the trait. *Alamosaurus,* for example, does not, at least so far as we know now. Unfortunately, very little is known of the skull in any titanosaurid. That holds true for most sauropods. They seem to have the unfortunate habit of losing their heads after they die. Sauropod skulls are very lightly constructed, and apparently that is the part of the skeleton that disintegrates first after death.

Perhaps the best information about what titanosaurid heads look like comes from the African species my colleagues and I named *Malawisaurus dixeyi* (ma-LA-we-SAWR-us dicks-EE-eye). The remains we have show that the cranium was domed and the snout very blunt. The nostrils were at the end of the nose, not raised to the top of the skull as in such long-headed forms as *Diplodocus.* Other differences from *Diplodocus* are seen in the teeth. They are a bit flattened in *Malawisaurus* and extend well back along the jaw rather than being limited to the front of the mouth.

There is no reason to think that the heads of all titanosaurid species looked alike. *Alamosaurus* did not necessarily have the same relatively small, round, beach ball–like head of *Malawisaurus*. We simply do not know what it looked like. On the other hand, the teeth of *Alamosaurus* are known, and they are rather pencillike cylinders of enamel. Whatever other differences or similarities there might be, the mouths of *Alamosaurus* and *Malawisaurus* were not exactly the same.

So how do we know *Alamosaurus* is a titanosaurid? There are several features that seem to characterize the family. The breastbones are large, the pelvis is broad. The vertebrae have several special attributes. Most importantly, the tail vertebrae join in a unique ball-and-socket joint that is only found in titanosaurids. Based on all of those characters, *Alamosaurus* is a titanosaurid. And based on features of the skeleton, *Alamosaurus* most closely resembles South American titanosaurids.

For all of the forty million years of the Cretaceous when sauropods were missing from North America, the titanosaurids were evolving, presumably happily, in South America. Although the South American land mass remained joined to Antarctica, it was essentially isolated by geography from the events of the rest of the world. South America was its own theater of evolution in which the major players were the species that were present there when South America became isolated. They were able to evolve in their own ways in response to the environmental conditions and chance circumstances in which they found themselves.

That is why dinosaurs from far-off places seem so strange. We are less familiar with them than we are with fossils closer to home. Faraway lands are generally less thoroughly searched for dinosaur fossils than North America, so new species are more likely to be found if a search is made. But there is nothing about faraway dinosaurs that is in any way more special than the more familiar dinosaurs. They have just evolved in a different theater of evolution. In the case of North and South America, the players from these two theaters became mixed when the Central American land bridge allowed dispersal between the two continents near the end of the Cretaceous.

South American sauropods provide an interesting case in point in dinosaur evolution. Not all South American sauropods are titanosaurids. To be sure, the South American titanosaurids seem strange relative to sauropods with which we are more familiar. *Saltasaurus* (SALT-uh-SAWR-us), for example, was a titanosaurid with big bony plates of armor in its skin. However, near the beginning of the Late Cretaceous, one South American sauropod seems weird from almost any perspective. *Amargasaurus* (uh-MARG-uh-SAWR-us) is its name. It has a double row of very long spines jutting up from its verte- brae. Other sauropods, for example *Dicraeosaurus* (dye-KREE-uh-SAWR-us) from Africa, are similar, but no other sauropod approaches *Amargasaurus* for length of spines. They are ungainly. Their purpose is unknown to me, al- though it has been suggested that the spines supported a sail. Given the vari- ety of vertebral structure seen in sauropod necks and backs generally, I think a more thorough understanding of their functional anatomy is called for before we can have confidence in our interpretations. Nevertheless, whatever *Amargasaurus* was doing with its spines, it seems to have been doing more of it, in a bigger way, than any other sauropod.

However, *Amargasaurus,* known only from South America, did not sur- vive through the Late Cretaceous. It went extinct without issue long before the end of the Age of Dinosaurs while titanosaurids flourished. Why?

The answer remains obscure. Titanosaurids may have had nothing to do with *Amargasaurus* and its fate, but it is clear that titanosaurids certainly had a different style of evolution than did *Amargasaurus.* In addition to their spe- cial traits, the evolution of South American titanosaurids brought about a diversity of species. *Amargasaurus* was bizarre while titanosaurids were di- verse. They filled the large-herbivore ecological niche in South America, pos- sibly even to the exclusion of other large herbivores of different families like *Amargasaurus.* In South America, during most of the time represented by the Late Cretaceous, titanosaurids were the dominant herbivores, without com- petition from big duckbills, horned dinosaurs, or other families of sauropods.

That is a far cry from the situation in the North American Late Creta- ceous. After sauropods were extirpated 105 million years ago, duckbills show up on the scene. Nowhere is that more clearly demonstrated than in the sec- ond world of Texas dinosaurs, where *Pleurocoelus,* the last sauropod before the gap, is found in the Glen Rose Formation but not much younger than that, and hadrosaurs are found in the Woodbine Formation, about 95 mil- lion years old. Horned dinosaurs do not show up in North America until later, just before the end of the Cretaceous.

Like *Alamosaurus,* horned dinosaurs and hadrosaurs tell us something about the intercontinental relationships of North American dinosaurs during the Late Cretaceous. In the case of horned dinosaurs, their ancestry can be traced to the Cretaceous Period of Asia, where *Protoceratops* lived. It was made famous by Roy Chapman Andrews and his expeditions to Mongolia earlier this century. Andrews and his group discovered the first dinosaur eggs. They belonged to *Protoceratops.*

Protoceratops and similar Asian dinosaurs are closely related to *Leptoceratops* and the more derived ceratopsids. Therefore, Asia is considered the evolutionary home of horned dinosaurs. They dispersed to western North America, evolving new species as they invaded new territory and adapted to new environments in the Late (but not very latest) Cretaceous. Their dispersal was facilitated by geography. The Western Interior Seaway was complete, and the western portion of North America was then a southerly extending peninsula of Asia. A similar biogeographic pattern is indicated for the duck-billed hadrosaurs, although they arrived in North America from Asia before the horned dinosaurs. Did these plant-eating invaders from Asia have anything to do with the sauropod hiatus in North America? Did they out-compete sauropods in the large-herbivore ecological niche?

At this point we simply do not have enough evidence to say with certainty how or if horned dinosaurs and duckbills might have contributed to the demise of sauropods in North America; however, we do know that other factors may have played a part in their mid-Cretaceous extirpation.

Staying with biological aspects for a moment, we know that the Lower Cretaceous flora of Texas, as shown by fossil plants in the Twin Mountains, Glen Rose, and Paluxy formations, was dominated by conifers and other gymnosperms even though flowering plants were present. In the Late Cretaceous, as shown by fossils from the Woodbine Formation, flowering plants became dominant. The change in plants correlates reasonably well with the change in herbivorous dinosaurs.

That is not necessarily surprising; in fact, we might expect things to be that way. Bear in mind that conifers did not die out totally; angiosperms simply became more prominent. The real question is whether both dinosaurs and plants were responding to other factors independently, or if the one was directly dependent on the other. We do not yet know.

However, we do know that at about the same time as the extirpation of the sauropods and the change in plants, the Western Interior Seaway was completed, radically changing the geography of North America. Bisecting a continent with such a major body of water is sure to have affected climate in significant ways by altering rainfall patterns and temperature. The changed geography also altered the routes by which animals might disperse. On top of that, recall that the Big Bend region did not become emergent until relatively late, and even after it did its environments continued to change as mountains were uplifted near the end of the Mesozoic. *Alamosaurus* was not in North America, so far as we know, when the horned dinosaurs and hadrosaurs got here. That is why *Chasmosaurus* and *Kritosaurus* are known from the Aguja Formation in Big Bend and *Alamosaurus* is not. You must wait until Javelina time before the new sauropod shows up. All of these factors must be considered in order to fully appreciate the complexity of the changing world of the Cretaceous Period, specifically between about 105 to 66 million years ago.

The suite of dinosaurs at Big Bend was diverse. So was the rest of the animal community. Not surprisingly, considering it was deposited along the coast, the Aguja Formation has a large number of species of cartilaginous fish: the sharks and rays. None is known from the Javelina, which was deposited inland by rivers as they flowed in their channels and when they overflowed their banks. Bony fish are present in each of the formations but are more diverse in the Aguja. Bowfins and gars are common to both. Among amphibians, salamanders are present in the Aguja but not the Javelina, and frogs are known from neither. It would be surprising for frogs to forsake streams and floodplain ponds, so we can predict that they will eventually turn up in the Javelina in all probability.

Among nondinosaurian reptiles, at least eight species of turtles are known from the Aguja while three have been reported from the Javelina. There is a champsosaur from the Aguja, a reptile similar in gross body form to alligators and phytosaurs. This is another example of convergent evolution to a semiaquatic, fish-eating lifestyle. A large marine mosasaur, the reptilian equivalent of a killer whale, is reported from the Aguja. Snakes and crocodilians are known from both formations. A pterosaur is known from the Javelina, and mammals are from both the Javelina and the Aguja.

Mammals have a particularly interesting story to tell. They are not especially diverse in either formation, but the species that exist there are informative. Specifically, marsupials are known from both. As we saw in the last chapter, marsupials are first known from Texas in the Woodbine Formation. Nowadays the state has a happy population of opossums, but on the whole, marsupials are most characteristic of South America and Australia. In South America today there is a diversity of opossum species, but throughout the Age of Mammals that continent sported a dizzying array of very strange marsupials. They evolved to fill all sorts of herbivore and carnivore niches that were filled by placental mammals in North America. The fossil record of Australia is less well known, but today that continent is noted for its marsupial kangaroos, koalas, and other odd mammals, including the egg-laying duck-billed platypus. How did such a distribution of mammals come about?

It is in part the result of the American free trade zone established near the end of the Age of Dinosaurs. While Africa and South America were conjoined in the middle part of the Cretaceous, marsupials and placentals were evolving in the northern hemisphere, isolated from the southern continents. At that time, Australia and South America were united in Gondwana, the conjoined southern hemisphere land masses. Africa was the first to rift out of the Gondwana pack, leaving South America connected to Australia through Antarctica. A remnant population of primitive mammals from earlier times evolved into the monotremes, or egg-laying mammals, like the platypus. Fossil monotremes are known from the Cretaceous of Australia and from early in the Age of Mammals of both Australia and South America. Now they are extinct in South America. They have never been found anywhere except those two continents, but we can infer that they once inhabited Antarctica because it formed the land bridge between South America and Australia during the Mesozoic Era.

We still have the problem of getting marsupials and even placentals down to the south. That happened very late in the Cretaceous. While *Alamosaurus* was dispersing northward from South America toward Big Bend, marsupials, at least, were heading south along with hadrosaur, hypsilophodont, and horned dinosaurs. Placental mammals probably followed shortly after. Once in South America, these mammals were able to disperse across the remnants of Gondwana. As the southern continents assumed their modern geography, the mammals evolved separately on each. This has given rise to the special distributions we see now, typified by kangaroos found only in Australia. It is, in part, a result of the Late Cretaceous free trade zone.

The mammals known from Big Bend are small. They are known by their teeth and little else. The teeth are small enough to sit on the head of a pin. However, the other extreme of the size spectrum is also seen at Big Bend, though not of mammals. *Alamosaurus* is the largest of the dinosaurs in North America during its time. *T. rex* is the largest North American carnivore of its day. There are two other examples of Texas giants found in Big Bend. These are really something to brag about.

When Barnum Brown and Erich Schlaikjer went to the Big Bend in 1940, before R. T. Bird traveled down from Glen Rose to meet them, they found the remains of a giant crocodile in the Aguja Formation. After it was shipped back to New York, the job of preparing the bones from the encrusting rock and restoring missing pieces fell to R. T. It was a real treat for him. The animal was huge. Can you imagine? A crocodile with a skull six feet long!

Brown's fossil work was funded by Harry Sinclair of Sinclair Oil, the company that used a brontosaur as its logo. There was talk of naming this crocodilian beast after him. Alas, that was not to be. The technical study of it was undertaken by R. T. and the great paleontologist Edwin H. Colbert. The Big Bend crocodile giant is now known as *Deinosuchus riograndensis*.

Since the time of Bird and Brown, more *Deinosuchus* has been recovered and more has been learned about crocodiles. The original reconstruction may not have been exactly right. The bone fragments have now been removed from the plaster of the reconstructed skull. It may be missing the real bits of bone, and it may not have been exactly correct, but it still looks pretty neat. Moreover, that original reconstruction is now a part of paleontological history. You can see it at the Dallas Museum of Natural History, its new home.

Deinosuchus was a shore and swamp dweller. It was master of its watery and damp environment the way carnivorous dinosaurs mastered the drier land. Like modern crocodiles in Africa, it may have lurked surreptitiously, smiling in murky bayous, dragging unsuspecting prey into the water as they drank or waded in the shallows. At two tons or more in weight, large *Deinosuchus* individuals may have preferred wading hadrosaurs to other kinds of prey.

Last but certainly not least, the other Texas giant at Big Bend is perhaps the most astounding of all. It is one of the most amazing animals of all time. It is a pterosaur, and it is the largest animal ever to fly under its own power. Its wing span approached forty feet, and it weighed as much as a good-sized person. The name of this beast is *Quetzalcoatlus northropi* (ket-zal-ko-AHT-lus NORTH-rop-eye) after the feathered serpent Aztec god.

The first specimen of *Quetzalcoatlus* was found in the early 1970s by Douglas A. Lawson, one of Wann Langston's students, who wrote the first announcement of it. It is Langston, however, who has provided the most insight into this exciting animal. The first specimen was part of a wing. Since it was found, a number of smaller individuals have turned up about twenty-five miles away. Assuming all the remains belong to one species, they provide a much more complete picture of *Quetzalcoatlus.* All the specimens come from the Javelina Formation at a level very near the end of the Cretaceous Period.

Pterosaurs are one of three groups of vertebrate animals that have achieved the ability to fly under their own power, not just glide. Birds, of course, are the most obvious. Bats are the second group, and they are an especially successful order of mammals. The third group is the pterosaurs, which are reptiles related to dinosaurs and birds but sharing a more distant common ancestor.

Pterosaurs are first known from the Triassic Period. There are some minute teeth from the Texas Dockum that are probably an early record of a tiny pterosaur. In the second world of Texas dinosaurs, pterosaurs are present but never common. The Glen Rose arm bone found with dynamite is somewhat similar in form to that of *Quetzalcoatlus. Coloborhynchus,* from the Paw Paw Formation, is an important record of crested-snout pterosaurs in North America. Specimens from the Antlers and other formations are problematic and not particularly informative as yet. The youngest record of pterosaurs is *Quetzalcoatlus* from Big Bend at the end of the Cretaceous. It shows us that pterosaurs died out near the great extinction that claimed the dinosaurs. Thus, in their long Mesozoic history, pterosaurs overlapped with birds for half or more of their existence. They did not overlap with bats, however, which come on the scene later during the Age of Mammals.

Flying is a demanding exercise that requires a high level of metabolic activity. Pterosaurs could maintain this level and were probably warm-blooded. They lacked feathers, but their skin may have been covered with fine fur, an insulation that helped prevent the loss of body heat. In all animals that fly, weight is a primary limiting factor. Various structural refinements evolved to make the skeleton both light and strong. In pterosaurs the bones are hollow, with very thin walls. Birds have light bones also, but with internal struts to provide strength. Bats, which have never reached the maximum size of birds or pterosaurs, have slim, gracile bones.

The evolution of wings occurred convergently in birds, bats, and pterosaurs. While the function of the wings for flight is the same in each, the structure of the wing is greatly different. In bats, the fingers of the hands are extremely lengthened. They serve as thin and delicate supports spaced through the stretched skin of the wing. In birds, the fingers are reduced, and most of the wing is made up of feathers. The leading edge is supported by the bones of the arm and the second finger. In pterosaurs, the bones of the fourth or ring finger are enormously elongate to support the leading edge of the wing. The wing membrane stretches from the fourth finger to the hind part of the body and from the first joint of the fourth finger to the neck.

Flight depends a great deal on having a properly shaped wing. It must be cambered with a convex upper surface, which induces air to travel faster over the wing than under it, thereby producing upward pressure or lift. In pterosaurs, the wing itself is a membrane of skin with collagen fibers running through it. The fibers probably functioned to strengthen the wing and helped control the shape of its edges.

The form of the inside of the skull in pterosaurs allows inferences to be made about the structure of their brains and the relative development of their senses. Their brains were large for reptiles of their size but were not quite up to a bird. They had a high degree of muscular coordination, which would certainly come in handy in aerial maneuvering or in takeoffs and landings. The sense of smell was probably poorly developed but the eyesight was very likely excellent, just as you would expect.

Given that all pterosaurs fly, the group as a whole displays a magnificent range of form expressed mainly in size, presence or absence of a tail, and in the skull. Pterosaur species are as small as a sparrow, as large as *Quetzalcoatlus,* and most all sizes in between. They can be divided into two groups based on the presence or absence of a tail. The more primitive of the two groups is thought to be that with the tail. A tail can function as a rudder, however,

Quetzalcoatlus, *the flying giant of Texas, the largest animal ever to take the air, had the wing span of a jet fighter. Illustration by Karen Carr.*

and that function is probably aerodynamically important for the species that have them.

The shape of the head varies greatly among pterosaur species. Some are rather blunt, but most are drawn out into a long beak. Some species have teeth, others are edentulous. Still others have teeth only toward the back of the mouth. Teeth are crowded in some species and widely spaced in others. There is much variation in the sizes of the teeth and also some variation in shape. Often the front teeth are procumbent, sometimes larger than the others. At least three species, none of them known from North America, were somewhat like flamingoes. They strained the waters of lakes and ponds for

The wings of bats, birds, and pterosaurs are not the same. In bats, which are mammals, the fingers elongate and skin is stretched between them. In birds, the number of bones is reduced, and they form a support at the front edge for the feathers that make up the wing. In pterosaurs, like Coloborhynchus *(shown here) and* Quetzalcoatlus, *the fourth or ring finger is enormously elongated to support the leading edge of the wing membrane. Illustration by Karen Carr.*

the minute crustaceans and other food particles that made up their diet. A flamingo turns its head upside down and forces water through the comblike edges of its beak to feed. The flamingolike pterosaurs used hundreds of long, narrow teeth along the jaw to comb the waters.

Most blatant about pterosaur heads, however, is the presence or absence of a crest and, if the species had one, the strange shape the crest might assume. We have already seen in chapter 3 the odd crest at the end of the snout of *Coloborhynchus* from the Paw Paw Formation. Other species had a crest in the middle of the snout, while still others had one at the back of the head. Famous *Pteranodon,* best known from Kansas, had a long crest at the back of its head equal in length to its long, pointy beak. These crests are most often

presumed to have an aerodynamic function, and perhaps they functioned to counterbalance the beak. They may also have been important in display.

In the case of *Coloborhynchus,* it has been suggested that the crest acts like a stabilizing keel when the animal dips its snout to catch fish. In fact, despite the diversity of skull shapes and teeth, most pterosaurs are thought to eat fish. The reason is that so many of the best-preserved pterosaurs were found in marine deposits, in rocks that were formed far out to sea from where the coastline was. Moreover, fish remains have been found in the stomach area of some pterosaur fossils.

Quetzalcoatlus lacked both a tail and teeth, but its jaws were long and pointed, and its skull is usually reconstructed with a small crest at the back. It is from the Javelina Formation, a rock unit deposited under floodplain conditions some 240 miles inland from the sea. It was the largest creature ever to fly above the Earth. How did it make its living in the Cretaceous world?

That is a tough question, and Langston has made some good suggestions that may answer it. First, it is reasonable to consider that *Quetzalcoatlus* was intimately associated with the Big Bend area rather than being a simple casual visitor. One bit of evidence toward that conclusion is the variety of the sizes of individuals found at Big Bend. Most ages in the population seem to be repre-sented. Masses of conifer needles or palm fibers were found with some of the smaller animals, perhaps suggesting a nest.

If *Quetzalcoatlus* lived in the area, what did it eat? There are a number of possibilities, but two stand out. First, it could have been a carrion eater. Why not? Vultures and condors achieve quite respectable size, including the record for the largest living bird in the world. They lack teeth as all modern birds do, but they can still strip flesh from a carcass. Their beaks, however, are not shaped like that of *Quetzalcoatlus.*

A second possibility for how *Quetzalcoatlus* might have fed is that it used its long beak to probe for invertebrates in the mud. Masses of fossil logs suggest that floods periodically struck the Javelina environment. The sedi-ments are highly burrowed. Perhaps *Quetzalcoatlus* stuck its slender beak into the sloppy substrate of flooded areas in search of molluskan meals. It is a possibility.

A half-sized flying model of *Quetzalcoatlus* with a wingspan of eighteen feet was built in the 1980s for an IMAX film called *On the Wing.* It weighed forty-four pounds and flew at thirty-five miles per hour. The model had a computer-controlled autopilot system that allowed the mechanical beast to flap its wings realistically and even to turn its head. However, lacking a tail, as Cretaceous pterosaurs did, it was hard to control. Several short flights of a few minutes each were made, but ultimately the thing crashed, as I guess we all do. Langston served as advisor to the project. To him the model seemed close to what the living creature would have been like. What a thrill it must have been to see a pterosaur fly, like a visitor from the past. The model has been restored and is now on display at the National Air and Space Museum in Washington, D.C.

Quetzalcoatlus is a true Texas giant, enigmatic and impressive. Ross Perot with a forty-foot wing span. But *Quetzalcoatlus* is not the only Texas giant. Big Bend, the third world of Texas dinosaurs, is home to four real giants in all: *Quetzalcoatlus; Deinosuchus,* the lurking crocodile with a hideous, insidious smile; *T. rex,* the meat-eating monster; and *Alamosaurus,* a docile plant eater and the largest of them all. Never before had Texas seen so many giants assembled in one place and never has it since. The other worlds of Texas dinosaurs had plenty to boast about in their own right. The second world, the heart of Texas dinosaurs, had *Acrocanthosaurus,* the meat eater, not much smaller than *T. rex;* and *Pleurocoelus,* the sauropod about the same size as *Alamosaurus.* The first world, during the Triassic, had no real giants, at least not any in the same size league as those which came later, but it had its own suite of oddities, not to mention Texas's first dinosaurs.

Looking back over all three worlds of Texas dinosaurs, it is clear that big changes occurred in the kinds of dinosaurs that were living in each and in the animals and plants that shared the landscape with them. But dinosaurs, as a group, survived all those changes. It was the one at the end of the Cretaceous that brought their downfall. That one, the Cretaceous-Tertiary extinction as it is called, marks the end of dinosaurs as we usually think of them in Big Bend, in Texas, and in the rest of the world.

The Cretaceous-Tertiary boundary in Big Bend is marked by a dramatic faunal change just as it is elsewhere in the world. After dinosaurs become extinct, mammals flourish. That is the most noticeable aspect of the faunal change. However, there is a change in the rocks that appears to coincide with the faunal change. The ancient soils formed in the early Tertiary, the initial period of the Age of Mammals, are different from the soils that formed while dinosaurs were around. The change in soils suggests that temperatures of the early Tertiary were cooler than in the Late Cretaceous and that there was higher rainfall. What could have caused that? Did these changes have anything to do with the demise of the dinosaurs? Those are perplexing questions that bring us to the edge.

What causes extinction?

CHAPTER 5

The Last Roundup

NOTHING IS MORE INTRIGUING as a concept or disturbing as a fact than extinction. Cynics may view today's demise of darters or spotted owls with ridicule, but one thing is certain: extinction is permanent. It cannot be undone. We will never be terrorized by yesterday's *T. rex* or *Alamosaurus, Jurassic Park* notwithstanding. That facet of dinosaur history—their extinction—is one fundamental reason why those long-gone beasts are so appealing: the extinction has already occurred, and it did not involve us. Dinosaurs exemplify not just the complete departure of a number of species but the total elimination of the rulers of the Earth. That starts hitting a little too close to home.

Mass extinction—the elimination of lots of different species, not just one or two—is even scarier. That is another reason why the demise of the dinosaurs is so intriguing. Lots of things, not just dinosaurs, appear to have gone extinct at about the same time. Mass extinction implies an ultimate, common, inexorable cause for the death of all afflicted species. But the immediate result is the same whether one species or a hundred goes extinct: each is dead. The definition of mass extinction is a matter of scale that makes a difference only if there is a fundamental, causal distinction between mass extinctions and the average rate of extinction throughout geologic time. Either way, extinction is the fate of most species.

We have seen that the fossil record of Texas is enough to demonstrate great changes throughout the reign of the dinosaurs. In their 160-million-year record, new dinosaur species evolved from more primitive ancestors while

An asteroid striking the ocean would cause a terrible tsunami. Some researchers see evidence for such an event in sediments deposited across the Cretaceous-Tertiary boundary, now exposed along the Brazos River. Illustration by Karen Carr.

other species died out without issue. Dinosaur extinctions were by no means limited to the end of the Cretaceous Period. They happened throughout the Mesozoic Era. The characters on the stage of evolution were constantly changing on the scale of geologic time. We can see that from fossils found right here in Texas.

It seems there is no single, imminent cause for extinctions in general, any more than there appears to be for the origination of new species. Evolutionary processes such as origination and extinction depend on the biological features of the organisms themselves, on the physical parameters of the environment, and on chance. These facets fit together to present the patterns of life history that we decipher from the fossil record. Thus, a given extinction is not necessarily like any other from the standpoint of what caused it. Therefore, it is necessary to examine a particular extinction event in its broadest context in order to fully understand it.

In the first world of Texas dinosaurs, during the Late Triassic Period, dinosaurs were not major players on the scene. They were minor members of terrestrial communities until faunal changes occurred, after which dinosaurs became more common. Two or more faunal changes occurred in the Late Triassic. For one of them, the cause has been attributed to a meteorite impact.

No dinosaurs of Jurassic age are known from Texas; however, the Cretaceous Period is rich in dinosaurs from its middle portion and from the end. The mid-Cretaceous dinosaurs are particularly important in demonstrating changes that took place approximately 100 million years ago. Although there is still room for argument and conjecture, it appears, as the Texas record stands now, that sauropods died out in North America (until the unrelated titanosaurid *Alamosaurus* appeared 40 million years later), other herbivores such as *Tenontosaurus* disappear, and *Acrocanthosaurus* is gone. New herbivores show up, most notably *Pawpawsaurus,* the nodosaur, and also duckbilled hadrosaurs. While the mid-Cretaceous dinosaur community was being rearranged, the Western Interior Seaway was being completed, and flowering plants were becoming more common relative to conifers and other gymnosperms. Climate, as influenced by the seaway and as it affected plants, plus the introduction of immigrant duckbills into North America from Asia appear to be major factors in the mid-Cretaceous faunal change and its accompanying extinction and local extirpation of several dinosaur species.

However, compared to what happened earlier in the Mesozoic, it is the terminal Cretaceous extinctions that are most enthralling because it was a dying of great magnitude. Not just the common dinosaurs but also many marine creatures went extinct, including mosasaurs and ammonites, some species of mollusks and plankton, and many other animals. But, of course, not everything died out. Frogs survived. Alligators survived. Turtles, snakes, and lizards survived. Birds survived, but not pterosaurs. Mammals made it through, then radiated evolutionarily into many spectacular and diverse species, filling niches once filled by dinosaurs and becoming the masters of the land. The selectivity of extinctions at the end of the Cretaceous Period is as puzzling in this example as it is in so many others. Nevertheless, it is this mass extinction that allows us to recognize the end of the Mesozoic Era—the Age of Reptiles—and the beginning of the Age of Mammals.

We know from the Big Bend fossil record that the dinosaur communities near the end of the Cretaceous consisted predominantly of horned dinosaurs and duckbills with their associated carnivores and other less prominent members of dinosaur society. Within this basic structure, while it was maintained for some time during the last stage of the Cretaceous, the species of dinosaurs changed with time as shown by the differences between the Aguja and Javelina formations. *Chasmosaurus* was replaced by *Torosaurus; Kritosaurus* was replaced by a different hadrosaur.

Looking at North America as a whole, the dinosaurs living near the end of the Cretaceous Period seem to have been distributed in three more or less distinct communities. In addition, we know that the Western Interior Seaway was retreating at the end of the Cretaceous, returning a terrestrial midsection to the continent, and that it was a time of active mountain building. Both of these factors profoundly influenced the geography and distribution of environments across North America. On top of that, we know that climate can be influenced by volcanic eruptions. The end of the Cretaceous was a time of massive outpourings of lava in India. It is against these and other regional backgrounds that we must view the terminal Cretaceous extinctions.

The terminal Cretaceous extinction event has become famous in recent years because it focused attention on collisions with extraterrestrial bodies as a cause for mass extinctions generally and as a major influence on the history of life periodically. Moreover, we have had the astounding opportunity to view an example of such a collision through the distance of space. No one who followed the trajectory of the comet Shoemaker-Levy to Jupiter in July of 1994 could help but be awed by the Earth-sized explosions that rocked the gaseous giant. Those explosions were caused by comet fragments smaller than that hypothesized for the terminal Cretaceous asteroid.

Meteorite and asteroid impacts supposedly initiate fundamental reorganization within ecological communities because they are presumed to catalyze the extinctions that remove selected species from Earth's biological system yet leave others to fill vacant ecological niches. Such impacts, while there is no question that they occur, are a matter of chance—good or bad luck, depending on your perspective, at least in the sense that nothing on Earth has any control over them. That adds an element of danger and immediacy to the mystery of dinosaur extinction. It could happen again. The same thing that happened to dinosaurs could, theoretically, happen to us.

Meteorites are masses of interplanetary rock and metal that fall to Earth. Asteroids come from a belt of planetoids located between Mars and Jupiter. Comets are like giant, dirty snowballs flying through space. When such masses strike the Earth, as they unquestionably do, they do so at great speed and with incredible force. Such a collision causes an explosion, the vaporization of rock, and the injection of dust into the atmosphere. If a meteorite were large enough, the results could certainly be devastating.

Evidence for an asteroid impact at the end of the Cretaceous comes first and foremost from the presence of anomalously high amounts of iridium, a metallic element related to platinum, first discovered in a thin layer of clay at the Cretaceous-Tertiary boundary in Gubbio, Italy. Similar iridium anomalies have since been found at the Cretaceous-Tertiary boundary at several places around the globe. Iridium is normally rare in rocks at the Earth's surface because most of the iridium that was here when the planet was formed has been incorporated into the deep interior of the Earth, depleting the amount in more superficial levels. That is not the case with meteorites because they were not subjected to the same processes that brought about the differentiation of the internal structure of the Earth. Therefore, meteorites contain much more iridium than the surficial rocks of the Earth. As the theory goes, when the asteroid struck the Earth and vaporized, the iridium it contained was distributed around the globe in the resulting explosion and dust plume. That is why, it is suggested, iridium is so concentrated in the boundary clay layer. High levels of iridium are the result of dust derived from the destruction of a large asteroid settling from the atmosphere. The only realistic alternative is that iridium may have been brought up from deep in the Earth by volcanic activity.

After the asteroid collided with the Earth, the skies filled with dust. Fires broke out across the globe, billowing smoke into the atmosphere. The sun's rays were blocked from the planet. Days became dark. With the sun shut out, temperatures plummeted. The cold and darkness took its toll on life. Plants and plankton suffered first. Because of their position in the food chain—the source of nourishment for so many animals—their misfortune became that of the community at large. Death came. Species went extinct.

The asteroid that struck the Earth at the end of the Cretaceous is estimated to have been about six miles in diameter and traveling at around fifty thousand miles per hour. It struck the Earth with the unimaginable force of 100 million megatons of TNT. That is three times the diameter and ten times the force of the Shoemaker-Levy comet fragments that struck Jupiter. Quartz crystals close to the asteroid impact site but not close enough to be vaporized or melted were shocked with a style of internal damage seen only at meteorite impacts and nuclear test sites. The crash carved out a crater 180 miles across. The crater has been located. It is called Chicxulub, Mayan for "tail of the devil," and it lies on the northern portion of the Yucatán Peninsula, extending out into the Gulf of Mexico. That is pretty close to home.

In Big Bend there are rocks that pass through the Cretaceous-Tertiary boundary from the Javelina Formation into overlying units. The boundary is recognized by the last occurrence of dinosaurs and associated animals like the pterosaur *Quetzalcoatlus* and by the first occurrence of mammals characteristic of the Cenozoic Era. The rocks show a change in soil development above the boundary compared to that below. This indicates a shift to a cooler and wetter environment, coinciding fairly closely with the extinction event. No iridium-rich layer has been found at Big Bend, but that is not necessarily surprising considering the locally haphazard processes of terrestrial sedimentation. It is more likely to find a layer anomalously rich in iridium in marine sediments where deposition is less variable.

At the end of the Cretaceous Period, Big Bend was dry but East Texas was not. It was under the sea. It is there, in marine rocks now exposed along a reach of the Brazos River in Falls County halfway between Waco and Bryan, that an iridium anomaly at the Cretaceous-Tertiary boundary can be found in Texas. However, much more than high amounts of iridium can be found there. The sediments of the Cretaceous-Tertiary boundary in Falls County are unusual. The Cretaceous marine rocks at the base of the section are scoured off to an irregular surface. In some of the higher remaining parts of the Cretaceous surface, a thin layer of waxy bentonitic clay can be found. Above that is a jumbled layer containing hunks of clay that were ripped off of the sea bottom. That is followed by sand and clay layers. Fossils of ocean-dwelling organisms in, above, and below these layers—plus other dating techniques and the abundance of iridium—suggest that this section of sedimentary rock represents what was happening at the Cretaceous boundary in a marine setting close to the site of the asteroid impact. The water on the continental shelf at this point was probably not more than about eight hundred feet deep and may have been as shallow as three hundred feet.

When the asteroid struck in Yucatán and the southern Gulf of Mexico, it caused a huge splash. It made a gigantic tsunami that circled the globe. Waves were so large that their turbulent waters scoured the ocean bottom for hundreds, even thousands, of miles around, churning and ripping up clay clasts and hunks of sea floor. As the energy of the tsunami waned, the mud and sand torn from the seabed began to settle rapidly. Large and small sedimentary particles were mixed together. They formed a jumble of clay, sand, and ripped-up sea bottom. That is what can be seen a thousand miles away from the impact crater along the Brazos River in Texas. A special name has been applied to storm deposits that look like this, and it applies to those sedimentary deposits produced by tsunamis and impact waves as well. The word is tempestite. What a great word. A tempestite is what we have in Texas, and it is quite possibly the direct result of a terminal Cretaceous asteroid impact.

An iridium anomaly, an impact crater, and a tempestite are not the same as a mass extinction. However, the fossil record in and around the tempestite in Texas can be examined for clues as to what is associated with the event that caused the tsunami. That has been done by Thor Hansen of Western Washington University and his colleagues. They found that prior to the impact event as evidenced by the tempestite, about one meter stratigraphically below it, there was a drop in the diversity of marine fossils. Moreover, abnormalities are evident in some of the ancient shells at that same level. Was something going on in the sea before the Cretaceous-Tertiary extinction event?

At the Cretaceous-Tertiary boundary there was an extinction of major proportions in marine organisms. In the Brazos Valley the rocks tell us that before the catastrophe, the kinds of mollusk species present—clams and their relatives—fed in the water column, mainly by filtering out food particles. In general, those organisms that lived or fed there suffered a greater die-off at the extinction than did bottom dwellers. After the event, there was a depleted fauna. Diversity remained low for some time after the extinction event, well into the Tertiary. Rather than feeding from the water column, a preponderance of the surviving molluskan fauna derived their nourishment from plowing through bottom sediments. In addition, measurements of Carbon-13, a form of elemental carbon, reveal a depletion through the same interval, suggesting that primary productivity in the ocean was reduced. If all that is true, it is consistent with the asteroid impact scenario of Cretaceous extinctions killing off primary producers in the ecosystem.

Is the asteroid scenario true? Is it compelling? Ahh, that is the problem. It may be reasonable, but it does not explain the drop in diversity or the abnormalities observed in fossils of marine organisms found in rocks dating just prior to the Cretaceous-Tertiary boundary along the Brazos. As far as dinosaurs go, even if there was an asteroid impact, we know that change through time is the rule, whether fast or slow. More importantly, we know that terrestrial faunas were changing before the time of asteroid impact.

Perhaps we can look at this issue another way. No one would deny that meteorites strike the Earth. We can even predict the statistical frequency at which large ones will strike the planet. We can search the heavens for one that might be heading this way. There was, in all likelihood, an impact event at the time of the Cretaceous extinctions.

No one would deny that if a collision of a meteorite with the Earth were powerful enough, it could end all life. And on the other hand, no one would deny that did not happen at the end of the Cretaceous. Lots of species survived the Cretaceous extinctions. As we have seen, whatever the cause, the extinctions were selective. We have also seen that the Western Interior Seaway was drying up, volcanoes were blowing in India, and something strange may have been happening in the oceans. So we are left with the problem of trying to determine the exact role, if any, of an asteroid impact within a complex of factors occurring at the end of the Cretaceous.

What causes extinction? Many things. Did an asteroid cause the extinction of dinosaurs? Maybe. Was it the primary cause? Nobody knows. Was it a major factor? Nobody knows that, either. We do not know if a possible aster-oid impact is of primary or secondary significance in the Cretaceous extinc-tions—or of no significance at all. Maybe its being at the end of the Creta-ceous is just a matter of coincidence. These are contentious issues.

So we do not know whether an asteroid impact caused dinosaur extinc-tion by and of itself or whether it was a minor factor that worked in concert with the conditions at the time. We do not know whether it had any signifi-cant effect at all because it is difficult to factor out other processes. We have only the barest of inklings as to how the process might work. I do not say that an asteroid impact was not the cause of Cretaceous extinctions, nor do I say all this to flaunt ignorance. Rather, it is a celebration of the fun of science. It should encourage those interested in fossils, perhaps contemplating a career in paleontology, who would like to find out for sure what happened and why. Only the beginning of the story has been written. It will be left to a budding young scientist to write the end. All that is required in scientific inference is that hypotheses be consistent with observations, that they be testable, and that the process of investigation be done honestly and in good faith.

Each extinction is a consequence of its time. Each mass extinction in Earth history is surrounded by a unique set of circumstances. These circum-stances combine for a synergistic effect that might become manifested in ex-tinction. Who knows what factor would push an already stressed ecosystem over the brink? Maybe an asteroid would do it.

There is an important lesson in this that becomes obvious from our knowl-edge of the changing Earth. Chance events that occur within the time sequence of physical and biological processes, once they occur, cannot be undone. Their effects on the living world at the time they happen are permanent. Those ef-fects are what is left to be acted upon by evolution in the future. If not buff-ered, the results are cumulative and additive. Once the asteroid hit, its dam-age—whatever it may have been to life on Earth—was done. Evolution went on from there, and here we are.

From a human perspective, the decisions we make concerning the hus-bandry of our planet have profound influence over some aspects of what will happen in the future and over most aspects of what can happen. We might build dams and generate electricity, but if appropriate actions are not taken, there will be no river that can support darters, and that means more than the loss of a little fish. If tropical forests are destroyed by clear-cutting, rainfall patterns will not be the same, and that means more than the loss of a few plant species. It all adds up to a mass extinction in geologic time—our geo-logic time—and that really is close to home. The current extinction event being suffered across the globe will affect us in ways we have not predicted.

The decisions of humans change the Earth and its life. Decisions concerning the management of water from the Edwards Aquifer in Texas, for example, will affect—positively or negatively—the survival of rare species, some of which are found nowhere else, and will determine the quality of natural resources that will remain for future generations. Illustration by Karen Carr.

The exact circumstances today are not the same as those that surrounded the Cretaceous-Tertiary boundary, but the lesson derived from studying mass extinctions whatever their circumstances are compelling indeed. Humans can impact the Earth with the same results as an asteroid collision.

After a mass extinction occurs, it seems that the meek inherit the Earth. Then the meek evolve, become more diverse, and ultimately are themselves not so meek anymore. Thus, mammals took over the world after the dinosaurs. But another group of survivors—the birds—deserves some credit for its success in the Age of Mammals.

The really fascinating thing about the efflorescence of birds in the Age of Mammals is that they can be considered surviving dinosaurs. How can that be? Birds are birds, and they do not look at all like *Torosaurus,* or *T. rex,* or *Alamosaurus.* It seems sort of hard to swallow that birds should be called dinosaurs because, as the British paleontologist Colin Patterson says, we have known what birds are forever, but we have been trying to figure out what dinosaurs are ever since their discovery. Maybe we should think of dinosaurs as a bunch of extinct birds. No matter what we call them, sauropods are not sparrows, and the use of either term—dinosaur or bird—for the whole suite expands the traditional concept of both these groups. The confusion comes from trying to express relationships among animals whose evolutionary branches split at a time when the ancestors were quite primitive and the descendants evolved to look very unlike each other. What do you call the whole group of related animals on different branches of the tree of life descended from a common ancestor near the trunk? In this case, you might call them birds or you might call them dinosaurs, but taken together, these animals form one natural group, whatever it is called.

The obvious and defining character of living birds is feathers. Most of their bodies are covered with feathers, except for their beaks and their scaly legs and feet. The feathers insulate their warm-blooded bodies and contour their shape for flight. Traditional, extinct dinosaurs lacked feathers so far as we know. Skin impressions are known from a number of main-line dinosaurs. There has even been a report of the impression of *Tenontosaurus* skin from Texas. A skin impression of *Chasmosaurus* is also known. All of the impressions that have come to light show scales, bumps, and nubbins, but no feathers. If we were to go no further in our analysis than that, we would conclude that birds are a special group, even if they do belong more inclusively with dinosaurs.

There is one important set of fossils from the Age of Dinosaurs that does show feather impressions. The fossils pertain to *Archaeopteryx* and are from 150-million-year-old rocks in Germany. *Archaeopteryx* is an early bird—the oldest, unless *Protoavis* from West Texas is accepted as a bird. The significance of *Archaeopteryx* is that it is a graphic connecting link between birds and dinosaurs. It has teeth, a long, bony tail, and fingers like dinosaurs, but it also has feathers and adaptations for flight. Detailed skeletal features of *Archaeopteryx,* modern birds, and dinosaurs suggest a close relationship among the three, implying that birds are a surviving branch of theropods.

An alternative hypothesis, however, proposes that birds are more closely related to crocodiles than to dinosaurs. Bird-dinosaur relationships seem better founded because the anatomical similarities are strongest between those two, most strikingly between theropod dinosaurs and birds.

The fossil record has brought to light some interesting biological features of the relationship between birds and dinosaurs. Birds are warm-blooded animals with high metabolic rates and rapid growth. They are active. Dinosaurs may have been similar. Bone growth occurs similarly in dinosaurs and birds but differently in mammals or lizards. That not only supports a close dinosaur-bird relationship, but it suggests that the rapid growth to adult size common to birds may also have been the norm for dinosaurs. If so, it would indicate a similar, warm-blooded metabolism. Additional research on fossil birds, however, shows lines of arrested growth in the bones of some ancient species. This indicates that there were differences between the growth patterns of some of the fossils and modern birds. Therefore, if growth pattern is dependent on metabolism, fully developed warm-bloodedness in birds may have evolved after feathers were already present.

Trying to infer physiological traits in extinct animals is tricky, but amazing progress has been made to that end. It is a growth industry in paleontology because we want to know what dinosaurs were like in life on the one hand and how birds got to be birds on the other.

Dinosaurs in their lifetimes had to do the same kinds of things birds do now in order to exist. They had to reproduce. In order to do that, they had to court, mate, obtain territory, build nests, lay eggs, incubate and hatch them, and finally care and train the young. Dinosaurs were animals of complex social structure that no doubt varied with the behavior of each particular species.

We have already utilized birds to interpret the lifestyles of several Texas dinosaurs. Ostrich behavior, for example, was used to make sense of the Proctor Lake hypsilophodonts. Young hypsilophodonts are thought to be precocial. They can run around soon after hatching, as quail do, because of the well-developed joint surfaces on their limb bones. The baby nodosaurid from the Paw Paw Formation is thought to be altricial, unable to wander away from the nest site, because its joint surfaces are less well developed. We can carry the comparison further and draw additional inferences because of other generalities about precocial and altricial birds. Precocial birds, as compared to altricial ones, usually have large eggs with a lot of yolk, big clutches of eggs, a long incubation period, a slower initial growth rate but relatively large young, and a high rate of attritional death. They also are less likely to remove shells from the nest site. Do these generalities hold for altricial and precocial dinosaurs as well?

Bird behavior requires sound and sight to accomplish such things as the

Archaeopteryx, a graphic connecting link between birds and dinosaurs, has feathers, but it also has teeth, a bony tail, three fingers on the hand, and other features showing that the birds may be considered a special group of theropod dinosaurs. Illustration by Karen Carr.

establishment and maintenance of territory, attracting mates, and rearing young. Bird song is among the most characteristic of avian attributes. Dinosaurs no doubt made noises, but it is unlikely they had a repertoire comparable to that of the avian world. The reason is that birds have a special kind of a voice box, called a syrinx, located deep in the throat where the two air passages leading to the lungs join. The syrinx works more or less independently on each side, in either air passage, to produce sound. Mammals like you and me have one larynx with vocal cords stretched in it, across which our breath flows to create mellifluous tones as we sing in the shower. Birds are able to produce more complex sounds because parts of the syrinx associated with the different air passages can work independently of each other. It is as if a bird can sing a duet with itself.

Moreover, the lungs of birds are quite complex. The high cost of flight in birds requires a continuous flow of air across the lungs to supply the body with oxygen. Birds do not have muscular diaphragms to facilitate breathing as mammals do. Respiratory efficiency is accomplished by a number of air sacs attached to the lungs. Some of these sacs extend into the hollow bones of the skeleton. One of the sacs surrounds the syrinx and helps produce sound. The anatomy of the syrinx and the sophistication of sounds produced varies among birds. Only a dinosaur with an anatomy similar to birds could sing in the same way they do. If any of the dinosaurs did produce noises like birds, they would probably be comparable to the less sophisticated sounds of the bird world.

That does not mean dinosaurs were silent: it simply means they made sounds in different ways. For example, some of the advanced duckbills had high, hollow crests atop their heads connecting their nostrils to their throats through wide tubes. These worked kind of like a tuba, reverberating with low notes audible over long distances. The same notes, however, were more difficult than high notes to pinpoint. While the melody was revealing to others of the same species, it was concealing to predators.

We do not know exactly what sort of noise each species made, but vocalization is a big part of behavior in general. It is very likely, then, that songs and cries were major factors in the social life of dinosaurs. The ancient Texas landscape must have echoed with dinosaur noises: the roar of *T. rex,* the bellow of *Pleurocoelus,* the low of *Tenontosaurus,* the honk of *Pawpawsaurus,* and the bleat of hypsilophodonts. Herds of *Chasmosaurus* may have grunted and mooed like herds of buffalo. *Troodon* and *Deinonychus* may have filled the night air with their barks like coyotes on the West Texas range.

Birds are often pretty flashy when it comes to color. Many bird species can afford to be conspicuously flamboyant because, even if they draw attention

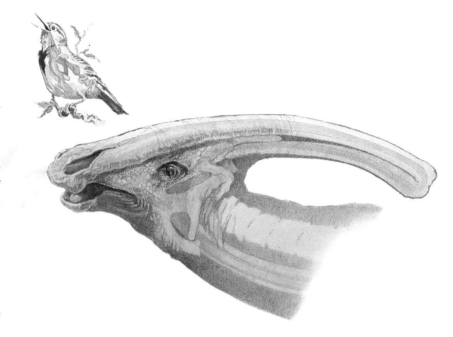

Birds have a special breathing design that keeps air flowing over the lungs. They also have a special voice box, a syrinx, that allows modern songbirds to produce complex sounds, as if one could sing a duet with itself. Dinosaurs almost certainly were not like that, although they were probably vocal. For example, the crests on advanced duckbills acted like a brass instrument to resonate sound. Illustration by Karen Carr.

to themselves, they are up in trees and can escape predators by flight. Ground-dwelling birds are more drab as a rule, with more prudent color patterns that help them hide rather than draw attention to themselves.

The color pattern of birds lies mainly in the feathers, which, judging from skin impressions, traditional dinosaurs did not have. However, many species of birds have pigmented skin. Red, blue, and yellow are common colors on naked patches of skin, such as the wattles of gobblers, the heads of cassowaries, or the inflated air sacs on the necks of prairie chickens. These splashes of color are useful in intraspecific interactions such as attracting mates.

We do not know about the color or the color patterns of dinosaurs. We have an artistic license to reconstruct them, but we also have a responsibility to be logical. In dinosaurs the skin, not hair or feathers, produced the color pattern. Some reptiles today have very colorful skin, and, as pointed out above, birds may have brightly colored skin patches. Mandrill baboons have shockingly colorful rumps and faces. However, I know of no color pattern so brilliant as that of Madagascan chameleons. Their skin screams in neon colors. I doubt dinosaurs were like that, but it is within the realm of possibility. I suspect dinosaurs exhibited a range of colors and patterns as do modern reptiles. Many lizards and snakes are very beautiful and quite colorful. Often the color is found in flashy patches—blue side bars and rosy throats—and is used in ways similar to the color patches in birds. They are important signals for communication during the breeding season. Similar patterns would be reasonable to expect in dinosaurs.

We might suspect that smaller species of dinosaurs—those more likely to become lunch if spotted by a carnivore—would maintain inconspicuous or camouflaging color patterns. Often these patterns change with age; for example, young alligators lose their mottling as they grow older and larger. Perhaps some young dinosaurs had better-defined color patterns than their parents. Larger species may have been generally less colorful than smaller ones. Males may have been more colorful than females, as is usually true in birds, in order to attract mates. Stripes may have adorned some dinosaurs, perhaps in species that formed herds like zebra or stalked the forests like tigers. We do not know for sure, but such patterns could be justifiable.

Although such aspects of dinosaur life as color, behavior, and song involve

Dinosaurs had the potential for a range of colors and patterns just like the ones modern reptiles show. Illustration by Karen Carr.

The author with his wife Bonnie, son Matthew, and daughter Melissa. Illustration by Karen Carr.

speculation, ultimately dinosaur interpretations go back to primary data: rocks, fossils, and observations of the modern world. Paleontological stories like this book are renderings of history—Earth history—and they must continually be revised. Paleontological stories never end because the science that makes them possible never stops. They are never-ending mysteries. Perhaps one of the most important features of paleontological stories, mysteries that they are, is that they are accessible and understandable. Paleontology is science for everyone.

Paleontology is also pure science. The value of fossils is in what they tell us, in the spark of curiosity they light inside almost everyone. That is what can be used to advantage in education. For those reasons alone, fossils are worth all the effort put into them. For those reasons alone, paleontology is worth pursuing.

The story of Texas dinosaurs is made up of a myriad of smaller tales, most of which have not been told, about everyday people who make one-in-a-million discoveries. People and fossils are juxtaposed in Texas. Much of the landscape, as we have seen, is rich in fossils of one sort or another. As the second most populous state, with some eighteen million residents, it is not surprising that a great number of excellent fossil finds have been made not by scientists but by people in other walks of life. Many of these finds were made quite by accident. People and fossils are brought together unconsciously at first, but for many Texans, paleontology becomes a calling.

There is a person behind each fossil discovery. We would not know nearly so much about the second world of Texas dinosaurs without the finds of Johnny Maurice and Thad Williams, who were kids when they made their discoveries. There is an agreeable landowner like James Doss, Philip Hobson, and Billy Jones behind most successful excavations in Texas. They are the heroes that allowed the science to be done. A book needs to be written just about the people who have found Texas fossils and helped bring them to light.

If dinosaurs had gone extinct without issue and were not related to birds, or if an asteroid had unquestionably and without complication caused the demise of dinosaurs in the Cretaceous Period, it would be easy to close the book on Texas dinosaurs. That is not the case. The story is continuing and will continue to grow. What we learn here is important elsewhere, and as more is learned in far-off places, we will gain a deeper understanding of the meaning of local fossils. The story of dinosaurs in the Lone Star State is an important piece in the puzzle of Earth history. That makes it all the more exciting.

Call me if you find something.

For Further Reading

Most of the references included in this list are advanced primary sources reporting the research on which the story of the Lone Star dinosaurs is based. However, I have included some references that are less technical. My objective is to provide a challenging source list for teachers and students. Although some references may be relevant to more than one chapter, they are listed only once.

CHAPTER 1. *Home on the Range*

Albritton, Claude C. 1942. Dinosaur tracks near Comanche, Texas. *Field and Laboratory* 1:160–80.

Albritton, Claude C. 1986. *The abyss of time.* New York: Freeman, Cooper and Co.

Alexander, Nancy. 1976. *The father of Texas geology, Robert T. Hill.* Dallas: Southern Methodist University Press.

Allen, Tom, Jane D. Allen, and Savannah Waring Walker. 1989. *Dinosaur days in Texas.* Dallas: Hendrick-Long Pub. Co.

Biffle, Kent. 1994. Kent Biffle's Texana: Following in footsteps of giants. *Dallas Morning News,* February 20, pp. 41A, 50A.

Bird, Roland T. 1939. Thunder in his footsteps. *Natural History* 43:254–61.

Bird, Roland T. 1941. A dinosaur walks into the museum. *Natural History* 47:74–81.

Bird, Roland T. 1944. Did *Brontosaurus* ever walk on land? *Natural History* 53:61–67.

Bird, Roland T. 1954. We captured a "live" brontosaur. *National Geographic Magazine* 105(5):707–22.

Bird, Roland T. 1985. *Bones for Barnum Brown: Adventures of a fossil hunter.* Ed. V. Theodore Schreiber. Fort Worth: Texas Christian University Press.

Colbert, Edwin H. 1961. *Dinosaurs: Their discovery and their world.* New York: E. P. Dutton & Co. (Plate 1 of this book is a photograph of the leg bone of an *Alamosaurus* from Big Bend.)

Cope, Edward Drinker. 1893. A preliminary report on the vertebrate paleontology of the Llano Estacado. *Geological Survey of Texas, Annual Report, 1892:*3–17.

Cummins, W. F. 1892. Report on the geography, topography, and geology of the Llano Estacado or Staked Plains. *Geological Survey of Texas, Annual Report, 1891:*129–223.

Dodson, Peter. 1990. Counting dinosaurs: How many kinds were there? *Proceedings of the National Academy of Sciences, USA* 87:7608–12.

Evans, Glen L. 1986. E. H. Sellards' contribution to paleoindian studies. In Holliday, Vance T., ed. *Guidebook to the archaeological geology of classic paleoindian sites on the southern High Plains: Texas and New Mexico.* College Station: Geological Society of America, 1986 Annual Meeting and Exposition, Department of Geography, Texas A&M University, pp. 7–18.

Farlow, James O., and Martin G. Lockley. 1989. Roland T. Bird, dinosaur tracker: An appreciation. In Gillette, David D., and Martin G. Lockley, eds. *Dinosaur tracks and traces.* Cambridge, U.K.: Cambridge University Press, pp. 33–36.

Hill, Robert T. 1901. Geography and geology of the Black and Grand Prairies, Texas. *U.S. Geological Survey, Twenty-first Annual Report,* pt. 7, 666 pp.

Hill, Robert T. 1937. Musings and mutterings about dinosaurs and dynamite . . . a stand-up strike. *Dallas Morning News,* March 14, pp. 7–8. (In this article Hill states that, to his knowledge, he collected the first known dinosaur remains from Texas in 1876. The fossil was found east of Millsap. Hill's field notes of his geological work east of Millsap were written in 1886 and include mention of his find. In his 1901 paper, he stated that he found the bones in 1886. While Hill probably did find the first dinosaur bones from Texas and may have found some earlier, I suspect that the 1876 date in the newspaper is a *lapsus* or a misprint and that the actual date that the first published dinosaur specimens from Texas were found conforms to the field notes; that is, 1886.)

Jacobs, Louis L. 1993. *Cretaceous airport: The surprising story of real dinosaurs at DFW.* Dallas: The Saurus Institute.

Kent, Dennis V., and Felix M. Gradstein. 1985. A Cretaceous and Jurassic geochronology. *Geological Society of America Bulletin* 96:1419–27. (This source places the end of the Cretaceous at 66.5 million years ago instead of 65. I follow this source because it makes a strong case for its conclusions.)

Langston, Wann, Jr. 1974. Nonmammalian Comanchean tetrapods. *Geoscience and Man* 8:77–102.

Langston, Wann, Jr., Barbara Standhardt, and Margaret Stevens. 1989. Fossil vertebrate collecting in the Big Bend: History and retrospective. In Busbey, Arthur B., and Thomas M. Lehman, eds. *Vertebrate paleontology, biostratigraphy, and depositional environments, latest Cretaceous and Tertiary, Big Bend area, Texas.* Guidebook, Field Trip nos. 1-A, -B, and -C. Austin: Forty-ninth Annual Meeting of the Society of Vertebrate Paleontology, pp. 11–21.

LDL Educational Resources Foundation. 1988. *Giants along the Paluxy.* Texas Parks and Wildlife, video tape.

Lessem, Don, and Donald F. Glut. 1993. *The Dinosaur Society's dinosaur encyclopedia.* New York: Random House.

Letson, Dawn. 1986. Robert Thomas Hill: A combative spirit. *Heritage News* (Summer, 1986): 6–9.

Murry, Phillip A. 1989. Geology and paleontology of the Dockum Formation (Upper Triassic): West Texas and eastern New Mexico. In Lucas, Spencer G., and Adrian P. Hunt, eds. *Dawn of the age of dinosaurs in the American Southwest.* Albuquerque: New Mexico Museum of Natural History, pp. 102–44.

Osborn, H. F. 1931. *Cope: Master naturalist.* Princeton, N.J.: Princeton University Press.

Shuler, Ellis W. 1917. Dinosaur tracks in the Glen Rose Limestone near Glen Rose, Texas. *American Journal of Science* 44(194):294–98.

Shuler, Ellis W. 1935. Dinosaur track mounted in the bandstand at Glen Rose, Texas. *Field and Laboratory* 4:9–13.

Shuler, Ellis W. 1937. Dinosaur tracks at the fourth crossing of the Paluxy River near Glen Rose, Texas. *Field and Laboratory* 5:33–36.

Udden, J. A. 1907. A sketch of the geology of the Chisos Country, Texas. *Bulletin of the University of Texas*, no. 93. Scientific Series no. 11, 101 pp.

Weishampel, David B., Peter Dodson, and Halska Osmólska. 1990. *The Dinosauria*. Berkeley: University of California Press.

Wilson, John Andrew. 1990. The Society of Vertebrate Paleontology 1940–1990, a fifty-year retrospective. *Journal of Vertebrate Paleontology* 10(1):1–39. (This paper contains photographs of Jack Wilson and E. C. Case's camp in the Panhandle in 1934.)

Winkler, Dale A., Phillip A. Murry, and Louis L. Jacobs. 1989. Vertebrate paleontology of the Trinity Group, Lower Cretaceous of Central Texas. In Winkler, Dale A., Phillip A. Murry, and Louis L. Jacobs, eds. *Field guide to the vertebrate paleontology of the Trinity Group, Lower Cretaceous of Central Texas*. Forty-ninth Annual Meeting of the Society of Vertebrate Paleontology, Austin. Dallas: Institute for the Study of Earth and Man (Southern Methodist University), pp. 1–22.

CHAPTER 2. *The Original Homestead*

Ash, Sidney. 1986. Fossil plants and the Triassic-Jurassic boundary. In Padian, Kevin, ed. *The beginning of the Age of Dinosaurs: Faunal change across the Triassic-Jurassic boundary*. Cambridge, U.K.: Cambridge University Press, pp. 21–30.

Ash, Sidney. 1989. A catalog of Upper Triassic plant megafossils in the western United States through 1988. In Lucas, Spencer G., and Adrian P. Hunt, eds. *Dawn of the age of dinosaurs in the American Southwest*. Albuquerque: New Mexico Museum of Natural History, pp. 189–222.

Auffenberg, Walter. 1981. *The behavioral ecology of the Komodo monitor*. Gainesville: University Presses of Florida.

Benton, Michael J. 1986. The Late Triassic tetrapod extinction events. In Padian, Kevin, ed. *The beginning of the Age of Dinosaurs: Faunal change across the Triassic-Jurassic boundary*. Cambridge, U.K.: Cambridge University Press, pp. 304–20.

Benton, Michael J. 1993. Late Triassic extinctions and the origin of the dinosaurs. *Science* 260:769–70.

Chatterjee, Sankar. 1983. An ictidosaur fossil from North America. *Science* 220:1151–53.

Chatterjee, Sankar. 1984. A new ornithischian dinosaur from the Triassic of North America. *Naturwissenschaften* 71:630–31.

Chatterjee, Sankar. 1985. *Postosuchus*, a new thecodontian reptile from the Triassic of Texas and the origin of tyrannosaurs. *Philosophical Transactions of the Royal Society of London*, ser. B, 309:395–460.

Chatterjee, Sankar. 1986. *Malerisaurus langstoni*, a new diapsid reptile from the Triassic of Texas. *Journal of Vertebrate Paleontology* 6(4):297–312.

Chatterjee, Sankar. 1986. The late Triassic Dockum vertebrates: Their stratigraphic and paleobiogeographic significance. In Padian, Kevin, ed. *The beginning of the Age of Dinosaurs: Faunal change across the Triassic-Jurassic boundary*. Cambridge, U.K.: Cambridge University Press, pp. 139–50.

Chatterjee, Sankar. 1993. *Shuvosaurus*, a new theropod. *National Geographic Research and Exploration* 9(3):274–85.

Colbert, Edwin H. 1970. A saurischian dinosaur from the Triassic of Brazil. *American Museum Novitates* 2405:1–39.

Colbert, Edwin H. 1989. The Triassic dinosaur *Coelophysis*. *Museum of Northern Arizona Bulletin* 57:xv + 160 pp.

Crompton, A. W., and J. Attridge. 1986. Masticatory apparatus of the larger herbivores during Late Triassic and Early Jurassic times. In Padian, Kevin, ed. *The beginning of the Age of Dinosaurs: Faunal change across the Triassic-Jurassic boundary.* Cambridge, U.K.: Cambridge University Press, pp. 223–36.

Galton, Peter M. 1986. Herbivorous adaptations of Late Triassic and Early Jurassic dinosaurs. In Padian, Kevin, ed. *The beginning of the Age of Dinosaurs: Faunal change across the Triassic-Jurassic boundary.* Cambridge, U.K.: Cambridge University Press, pp. 203–21.

Hodych, J. P., and G. R. Dunning. 1992. Did the Manicouagan impact trigger end-of-Triassic mass extinction? *Geology* 20:51–54.

Hunt, Adrian P. 1989. A new ?ornithischian dinosaur from the Bull Canyon Formation (Upper Triassic) of east-central New Mexico. In Lucas, Spencer G., and Adrian P. Hunt, eds. *Dawn of the age of dinosaurs in the American Southwest.* New Mexico Museum of Natural History, pp. 355–58.

Jacobs, Louis L., and Phillip A. Murry. 1980. The vertebrate community of the Triassic Chinle Formation near St. Johns, Arizona. In Jacobs, Louis L., ed. *Aspects of vertebrate history: Essays in honor of Edwin Harris Colbert.* Flagstaff: Museum of Northern Arizona Press, pp. 55–71.

Lehman, Thomas M. 1994. The saga of the Dockum Group and the case of the Texas/New Mexico boundary fault. *New Mexico Bureau of Mines and Mineral Resources Bulletin* 150:37–51.

Long, Robert A., and Phillip A. Murry. 1995. Late Triassic (Carnian and Norian) tetrapods from the southwestern United States. Albuquerque: New Mexico Museum of Natural History, Bulletin 4.

Lucas, Spencer G., and Zhexi Luo. 1993. *Adelobasileus* from the Upper Triassic of West Texas: The oldest mammal. *Journal of Vertebrate Paleontology* 13(3):309–34.

Murry, Phillip A. 1986. Vertebrate paleontology of the Dockum Group: Western Texas and eastern New Mexico. In Padian, Kevin, ed. *The beginning of the Age of Dinosaurs: Faunal change across the Triassic-Jurassic boundary.* Cambridge, U.K.: Cambridge University Press, pp. 109–37.

Olsen, Paul E., and Hans-Dieter Sues. 1986. Correlation of continental Late Triassic and Early Jurassic sediments, and patterns of the Triassic-Jurassic tetrapod transition. In Padian, Kevin, ed. *The beginning of the Age of Dinosaurs: Faunal change across the Triassic-Jurassic boundary.* Cambridge, U.K.: Cambridge University Press, pp. 321–51.

Padian, Kevin. 1990. The ornithischian form genus *Revueltosaurus* from the Petrified Forest of Arizona (Late Triassic: Norian; Chinle Formation). *Journal of Vertebrate Paleontology* 10(2):268–69.

Rogers, Raymond R., C. C. Swisher III, Paul C. Sereno, A. M. Monetta, C. A. Forster, and R. N. Martinez. 1993. The Ischigualasto tetrapod assemblage (Late Triassic, Argentina) and 40 Ar/39 Ar dating of dinosaur origins. *Science* 260:794–97.

Schwartz, Hilde L., and David D. Gillette. In press. Geology and taphonomy of the *Coelophysis* Quarry, Upper Triassic Chinle Formation, Ghost Ranch, New Mexico. *Journal of Paleontology.*

Sereno, Paul C. 1991. *Lesothosaurus*, "Fabrosaurids," and the early evolution of Ornithischia. *Journal of Vertebrate Paleontology* 11(2):168–97.

Sereno, Paul C. 1991. Basal archosaurs: Phylogenetic relationships and functional implications. *Journal of Vertebrate Paleontology* 11, supplement to no. 4, 53 pp.

Sereno, Paul C., C. A. Forster, Raymond R. Rogers, and A. M. Monetta. 1993. Primitive dinosaur skeleton from Argentina and the early evolution of Dinosauria. *Nature* 361:64–66.

Sereno, Paul C., and Fernando E. Novas. 1992. The complete skull and skeleton of an early dinosaur. *Science* 258:1137–40.

Small, Bryan. 1989. Post Quarry. In Lucas, Spencer G., and Adrian P. Hunt, eds. *Dawn of the age of dinosaurs in the American Southwest.* New Mexico Museum of Natural History, pp. 145–48.

Sues, Hans-Dieter. 1991. Venom-conducting teeth in a Triassic reptile. *Nature* 351:141–43.

Weigelt, Johannes. 1989. Recent vertebrate carcasses and their paleobiological implications. Chicago: University of Chicago Press. (This is a translation by Judith Schaefer, with a foreword by Anna K. Behrensmeyer and Catherine Badgley, of *Rezente Wirbeltierleichen und ihre paläobiologische Bedeutung,* published by Weigelt in 1927.)

CHAPTER 3. *The Heart of Texas Dinosaurs*

Barck, Alan. 1992. Paleontology of the Glen Rose Formation (Lower Cretaceous), Hood County, Texas. *Texas Journal of Science* 44(1):3–24.

Bertram, Brian C. R. 1992. *The ostrich communal nesting system.* Princeton, N.J.: Princeton University Press.

Coombs, Walter P., Jr. In press. A new nodosaurid ankylosaur (Dinosauria: Ornithischia) from the Lower Cretaceous of Texas. *Journal of Vertebrate Paleontology.*

Farlow, James O. 1981. Estimates of dinosaur speeds from a new trackway site in Texas. *Nature* 294:747–48.

Farlow, James O. 1993. *The dinosaurs of Dinosaur Valley State Park.* Austin: Texas Parks and Wildlife Department.

Farlow, James O., Jeffrey G. Pittman, and J. Michael Hawthorne. 1989. *Brontopodus birdi* Lower Cretaceous sauropod footprints from the U.S. Gulf coastal plain. In Gillette, David D., and Martin G. Lockley, eds. *Dinosaur tracks and traces.* Cambridge, U.K.: Cambridge University Press, pp. 371–94.

Gallup, Marc R. 1989. Functional morphology of the hindfoot of the Texas sauropod *Pleurocoelus* sp. indet. *Geological Society of America,* Special Paper, 238:71–74.

Godfrey, Laurie R., and John R. Cole. 1986. Blunder in their footsteps. *Natural History* 95(8):5–12.

Hastings, R. J. 1989. New observations on Paluxy River tracks confirm their dinosaurian origin. *Journal of Geological Education* 35(1):4–15.

Hawthorne, J. Michael. 1990. Dinosaur track-bearing strata of the Lampasas Cut Plain and Edwards Plateau, Texas. *Baylor Geological Studies* 49:1–17.

Hurxthal, Lewis M. 1986. Our gang, ostrich style. *Natural History* 95(12):34–41.

Jacobs, Bonnie Fine. 1989. Paleobotany of the Lower Cretaceous Trinity Group, Texas. In Winkler, Dale A., Phillip A. Murry, and Louis L. Jacobs, eds. *Field guide to the vertebrate paleontology of the Trinity Group, Lower Cretaceous of Central Texas.* Forty-ninth Annual Meeting of the Society of Vertebrate Paleontology, Austin. Dallas: Institute for the Study of Earth and Man (Southern Methodist University), pp. 31–33.

Jacobs, Louis L., Dale A. Winkler, and Phillip A. Murry. 1989. Modern mammal origins: Evolutionary grades in the Early Cretaceous of North America. *Proceedings of the National*

Academy of Sciences, USA 86:4992–95.

Jacobs, Louis L., Dale A. Winkler, and Phillip A. Murry. 1991. On the age and correlation of Trinity mammals, Early Cretaceous of Texas, USA. *Newsletter on Stratigraphy* 24(1/2):35–43.

Jacobs, Louis L., Dale A. Winkler, Phillip A. Murry, and John M. Maurice. 1994. A nodosaurid scuteling from the Texas shore of the Western Interior Seaway. In Carpenter, K., and John R. Horner, eds. *Dinosaur eggs and babies.* Cambridge, U.K.: Cambridge University Press, pp. 337–46.

Kirkland, James I. Predation of dinosaur nests by terrestrial crocodilians. In Carpenter, K., and John R. Horner, eds. *Dinosaur eggs and babies.* Cambridge, U.K.: Cambridge University Press, pp. 124–33.

Kuban, Glen J. 1989. Elongate dinosaur tracks. In Gillette, David D., and Martin G. Lockley, eds. *Dinosaur tracks and traces.* Cambridge, U.K.: Cambridge University Press, pp. 57–72.

Kuban, Glen J. 1989. Color distinctions and other curious features of dinosaur tracks near Glen Rose, Texas. In Gillette, David D., and Martin G. Lockley, eds. *Dinosaur tracks and traces.* Cambridge, U.K.: Cambridge University Press, pp. 427–40.

Lee, Yuong-Nam. In press. A new nodosaurid ankylosaur (Dinosauria: Ornithischia) from the Paw Paw Formation (Late Albian) of Texas. *Journal of Vertebrate Paleontology.*

Lockley, Martin G. 1991. *Tracking dinosaurs: A new look at an ancient world.* Cambridge, U.K.: Cambridge University Press.

Murry, Phillip A., Dale A. Winkler, and Louis L. Jacobs. 1991. An azhdarchid pterosaur humerus from the Lower Cretaceous Glen Rose Formation of Texas. *Journal of Paleontology* 65(1):167–70.

Parris, David C., and Joan Echols. 1992. The fossil bird *Ichthyornis* in the Cretaceous of Texas. *Texas Journal of Science* 44(2):201–12.

Pittman, Jeffrey G. 1989. Stratigraphy, lithology, depositional environment, and track type of dinosaur track-bearing beds of the Gulf coastal plain. In Gillette, David D., and Martin G. Lockley, eds. *Dinosaur tracks and traces.* Cambridge, U.K.: Cambridge University Press, pp. 135–53.

Pittman, Jeffrey G. 1990. Dinosaur tracks and track beds in the middle part of the Glen Rose Formation, western Gulf basin, USA. In Bergan, Gail R., and Jeffrey G. Pittman, eds. *Near-shore clastic-carbonate facies and dinosaur trackways in the Glen Rose Formation (Lower Cretaceous) of Central Texas.* Field Trip no. 8. Dallas: Geological Society of America Annual Meeting, pp. 47–83.

Stovall, J. Willis, and Wann Langston, Jr. 1950. *Acrocanthosaurus atokensis,* a new genus and species of Lower Cretaceous Theropoda from Oklahoma. *American Midland Naturalist* 43:696–728.

Winkler, Dale A., and Phillip A. Murry. 1989. Paleoecology and hypsilophodontid behavior at the Proctor Lake dinosaur locality (Early Cretaceous), Texas. *Geological Society of America,* Special Paper, 238:55–61.

Winkler, Dale A., Phillip A. Murry, and Louis L. Jacobs. 1990. Early Cretaceous (Comanchean) vertebrates of Central Texas. *Journal of Vertebrate Paleontology* 10(1):95–116.

Winkler, Dale A., Phillip A. Murry, and Louis L. Jacobs. Submitted. A primitive *Tenontosaurus* (Ornithopoda: Dinosauria) from the Early Cretaceous of Texas.

Winkler, Dale A., Phillip A. Murry, Louis L. Jacobs, William R. Downs, J. Russell Branch, and Patrick Trudell. 1988. The Proctor Lake dinosaur locality, Lower Cretaceous of Texas. *Hunteria* 2(5):1–8.

CHAPTER 4. *The Land of Texas Giants*

Brown, Barnum. 1942. The largest known crocodile. *Natural History* 49:260–61.

Carpenter, Kenneth. 1990. Variation in *Tyrannosaurus rex.* In Carpenter, K., and Philip J. Currie, eds. Dinosaur systematics: Approaches and perspectives. Cambridge, U.K.: Cambridge University Press, pp. 141–45.

Colbert, Edwin H., and Roland T. Bird. 1954. A gigantic crocodile from the Upper Cretaceous beds of Texas. *American Museum Novitates* 1688:1–22.

Davies, Kyle L., and Thomas M. Lehman. 1989. The WPA Quarries. In Busbey, Arthur B., and Thomas M. Lehman, eds. *Vertebrate paleontology, biostratigraphy, and depositional environments, latest Cretaceous and Tertiary, Big Bend area, Texas.* Guidebook, Field Trip nos. 1-A, -B and -C. Austin: Forty-ninth Annual Meeting of the Society of Vertebrate Paleontology, pp. 32–42.

Forster, Catherine A., Paul C. Sereno, Thomas W. Evans, and Timothy Rowe. 1993. A complete skull of *Chasmosaurus mariscalensis* (Dinosauria: Ceratopsidae) from the Aguja Formation (Late Campanian) of West Texas. *Journal of Vertebrate Paleontology* 13(2):161–70.

Jacobs, Louis L. 1993. *Quest for the African dinosaurs.* New York: Villard Books.

Jacobs, Louis L., Dale A. Winkler, William R. Downs, and Elizabeth M. Gomani. 1993. New material of an Early Cretaceous titanosaurid sauropod dinosaur from Malawi. *Palaeontology* 36(3):523–34.

Langston, Wann, Jr. 1981. Pterosaurs. *Scientific American* 244(2):122–36.

Lawson, Douglas A. 1975. Pterosaur from the latest Cretaceous of West Texas: Discovery of the largest flying creature. *Science* 187:947–48.

Lawson, Douglas A. 1976. *Tyrannosaurus* and *Torosaurus,* Maestrichtian dinosaurs from Trans-Pecos, Texas. *Journal of Paleontology* 50(1):158–64.

Lehman, Thomas M. 1987. Late Maastrichtian paleoenvironments and dinosaur biogeography in the western interior of North America. *Palaeogeography, Palaeoclimatology, Palaeoecology* 60:189–217.

Lehman, Thomas M. 1989. *Chasmosaurus mariscalensis,* sp. nov., a new ceratopsian dinosaur from Texas. *Journal of Vertebrate Paleontology* 9(2):137–62.

Lehman, Thomas M. 1989. Upper Cretaceous (Maastrichtian) paleosols in Trans-Pecos Texas. *Geological Society of America Bulletin* 101:188–203.

Lehman, Thomas M. 1989. Overview of Late Cretaceous sedimentation in Trans-Pecos Texas. In Busbey, Arthur B., and Thomas M. Lehman, eds. *Vertebrate paleontology, biostratigraphy, and depositional environments, latest Cretaceous and Tertiary, Big Bend area, Texas.* Guidebook, Field Trip nos. 1-A, -B and -C. Austin: Forty-ninth Annual Meeting of the Society of Vertebrate Paleontology, pp. 23–25.

Lehman, Thomas M. 1990. The ceratopsian subfamily Chasmosaurinae: Sexual dimorphism and systematics. In Carpenter, K., and Philip J. Currie, eds. *Dinosaur systematics: Approaches and perspectives.* Cambridge, U.K.: Cambridge University Press, pp. 211–29.

Lehman, Thomas M. 1990. Paleosols and the Cretaceous/Tertiary transition in the Big Bend region of Texas. *Geology* 18:362–64.

Lehman, Thomas M. 1991. Sedimentation and tectonism in the Laramide Tornillo Basin of West Texas. *Sedimentary Geology* 75:9–28.

Maxwell, Ross A., John T. Lonsdale, Roy T. Hazzard, and John A. Wilson. 1967. *Geology of Big Bend National Park, Brewster County, Texas.* Publication 6711. Austin: University of Texas, Bureau of Economic Geology.

Pascual, Rosendo, et al. 1992. First discovery of monotremes in South America. *Nature* 356:704–706.

Rohr, D. M., A. J. Boucot, J. Miller, and M. Abbott. 1986. Oldest termite nest from the Upper Cretaceous of West Texas. *Geology* 14:87–88.

Wellnhofer, Peter. 1991. *The illustrated encyclopedia of pterosaurs.* New York: Crescent Books.

Wheeler, E. A., Thomas M. Lehman, and P. E. Gasson. 1994. *Javelinoxylon,* an Upper Cretaceous dicotyledonous tree from Big Bend National Park, Texas, with presumed malvalean affinities. *American Journal of Botany* 81(16):703–10.

CHAPTER 5. *The Last Roundup*

Albritton, Claude C., Jr. 1989. *Catastrophic episodes in Earth history.* London: Chapman and Hall.

Alcorn, Gordon D. 1991. *Birds and their young.* Harrisburg, Pa.: Stackpole Books.

Alvarez, L. W., Walter Alvarez, Frank Asaro, and H. V. Michel. 1980. Extraterrestrial cause for the Cretaceous-Tertiary extinction. *Science* 208:1095–1108.

Alvarez, Walter, and Frank Asaro. 1990. An extraterrestrial impact. *Scientific American* (October, 1990):78–84.

Archibald, J. David. 1992. Myths, theories, and facts of dinosaur extinction. In Preiss, B., R. Silverberg, and M. Greenberg, eds. *The ultimate dinosaur.* New York: Byron Preiss Visual Pub., pp. 276–88.

Barreto, Claudia, Ralph M. Albrecht, Dale E. Bjorling, John R. Horner, and Norman J. Wilsman. 1993. Evidence of the growth plate and the growth of long bones in juvenile dinosaurs. *Science* 262:2020–23.

Bourgeois, J., Thor A. Hansen, P. L. Wiberg, and E. G. Kauffman. 1988. A tsunami deposit at the Cretaceous-Tertiary boundary in Texas. *Science* 241:567–70.

Brooke, Michael, and Tim Birkhead. 1991. *The Cambridge encyclopedia of ornithology.* Cambridge, U.K.: Cambridge University Press.

Carpenter, K., and John R. Horner, eds. 1994. *Dinosaur eggs and babies.* Cambridge, U.K.: Cambridge University Press.

Chinsamy, Anusuya, Luis M. Chiappe, and Peter Dodson. 1994. Growth rings in Mesozoic birds. *Nature* 368:196–97.

Courtillot, Vincent E. 1990. A volcanic eruption. *Scientific American* (October, 1990):85–92.

Ganapathy, R., S. Gartner, and M. J. Jiang. 1981. Iridium anomaly at the Cretaceous-Tertiary boundary in Texas. *Earth and Planetary Science Letters* 54:393–96.

Greenewalt, C. H. 1968. How birds sing. *Scientific American* 221:126–39.

Hansen, Thor A., R. B. Farrand, H. A. Montgomery, H. G. Billman, and G. Blechschmidt. 1987. Sedimentology and extinction patterns across the Cretaceous-Tertiary boundary interval in East Texas. *Cretaceous Research* 8:229–52.

Hansen, Thor A., Benjamin R. Farrell, and Banks Upshaw III. 1993. The first two million years after the Cretaceous-Tertiary boundary in East Texas: Rate and paleoecology of the molluscan recovery. *Paleobiology* 19(2):251–65.

Hansen, Thor A., Banks Upshaw III, Erle G. Kauffman, and Wulf Gose. 1993. Patterns of molluscan extinction and recovery across the Cretaceous-Tertiary boundary in East Texas:

Report on new outcrops. *Cretaceous Research* 14:685–706.

Hildebrand, Alan R., et al. 1991. Chicxulub Crater: A possible Cretaceous/ Tertiary boundary impact crater on the Yucatán Peninsula, Mexico. *Geology* 19:867–71.

Nowicki, S. 1987. Vocal tract resonances in oscine bird sound production: Evidence from bird songs in a helium atmosphere. *Nature* 325:53–55.

Padian, Kevin, ed. 1986. The origin of birds and the evolution of flight. *Memoirs of the California Academy of Sciences* 8.

Patterson, Colin. 1993. Naming names. *Nature* 366:518.

Rampino, Michael R., Stephen Self, and Richard B. Strothers. 1988. Volcanic winters. *Annual Review of Earth and Planetary Science* 16:73–99.

Raup, David M. 1991. *Extinction: Bad genes or bad luck?* New York: W. W. Norton & Co.

Short, Lester L. 1993. *The lives of birds.* New York: Henry Holt and Co.

Stanley, Steven M. 1994. Extinctions; or, which way did they go? *Earth: The science of our planet.* New York: Wm. C. Brown Pub., pp.106–15.

Stanley, Steven M. 1987. *Extinction.* New York: Scientific American Library.

Ward, Peter. 1994. *The end of evolution: On mass extinctions and the preservation of biodiversity.* New York: Bantam Books.

Weishampel, David B. 1981. Acoustic analysis of potential vocalization in lambeosaurine dinosaurs (Reptilia: Ornithischia). *Paleobiology* 7:252–61.

Wellnhofer, Peter. 1991. *Archaeopteryx.* In Mock, Douglas W., ed. *Behavior and evolution of birds: Readings from Scientific American magazine.* New York: W. H. Freeman and Co., pp. 153–64.

Index